The Splendour of Italy

354 COLOUR PICTURES AND 8 COLOUR PLATES

Venice. Rialto Bridge.

STORTI EDIZIONI srl.

ITALY

Italy is a peninsula in the Mediterranean Sea, divided from northern Europe by the Alpine mountain range, while in the south it extends towards Africa. Its temperate climate and geographical position made it a land of conquest and many peoples settled here leaving traces of their passage. Italy can be divided into three large basins: the North from the Alps to the Apennines, where architecture, sculpture and painting refer to the migrations coming from northern Europe and the Balkans; the Centre, where the Etruscans gave rise to the Italian civilisation; the South strewn with ruins of colonies of Greek and Mediterranean origin that were established there.

The journey of the "Splendour of Italy" begins in Venice, rising from its foundations in the silt of the lagoon, where it fostered an incomparable civilisation. It continues in Florence, the cradle of Humanism adopted by the Western world; and in Rome, the city that has existed for two thousand years and that has enlightened the world with its Empire and the Papacy; in Naples, the capital of the South, and Pompeii, where the flow of lava from Vesuvius in 79 A.D brought life to a sudden end, catching its inhabitants in their last moments; in Sicily, the island of fire, temples and indescribable scenery, rich with remnants of ancient civilisations. And it ends with the numerous other islands, with vestiges of cultures that remain unknown even today.

Florence. Piazza della Signoria.

Rome. St. Peter's Square and Basilica.

Florence. Academy.
David by Michelangelo.

Sicily, Agrigento.
Temple of Concord.

Venice. Bridge of Sighs.

Naples. Landscape

Naples, National Archaeological Museum. Faun statue.

National Museum of Reggio Calabria. Riace bronzes.

Venice

During the barbarian invasions the Venetians abandoned the mainland and settled on the islands in the lagoon, extending their trade routes to the Greek coastline and the Levant. After the establishment of the first settlements, the inhabitants of Rialto built a church in honour of the patron saint, St. Mark, a Doges' Palace and an Arsenal, constructed opposite one of the entrances to the lagoon to the east facing the sea. Many doges experienced in the art of commerce and in relations with the other powers, followed one anoth-

St. Mark's Basin.

er in the government in Rialto. At the end of the 12th century, Enrico Dandolo, a leading figure who defended the interests of Rialto so boldly that the Emperor, Manuel Comnenus, had him blinded, was elected. The Fourth Crusade (1202-1204) assembled 33,500 crusaders and 4,500 horses on the island of the Lido of Venice to set sail to conquer the Holy Sepulchre. Enrico Dandolo had fixed the cost of transportation and supplies at 75,000 marks for a period of two years. The Crusaders accepted but were not able to collect the fixed amount. Then the plague began to spread among their ranks gathered at the Lido and Doge Enrico Dandolo ordered them not to leave until the agreed amount had been obtained. The Crusaders gave in and Enrico Dandolo led them to conquer Zara, and later Constantinople, which fell under the command of the ninety-year old Doge, the first to enter the city. Venice was offered *a quarter and half of the Empire of Romania*. The remains of Enrico Dandolo are said to be still in Constantinople in the Basilica of Santa Sophia.

St. Mark's Square

RELIGIOUS CENTRE

...the landing place without equal,
the incredible composition
of fantastic architecture...

Thomas Mann,
Death in Venice.

St. Mark's Square flooded by 'acqua alta'.

Venetian lagoon. Landscape.

Old map of Venice.

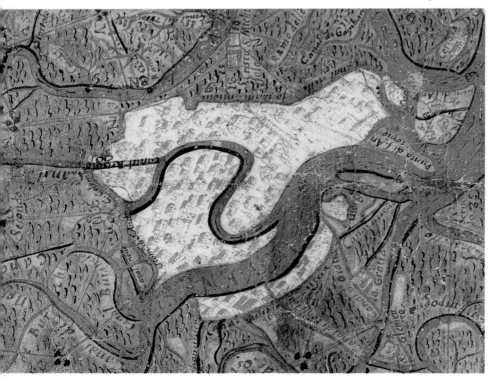

The recorded history of Venice goes back over one thousand years. Life on the archipelago of Rivoalto already existed before the government, in 810, transferred its seat from Malamocco, on the Adriatic shore to the lagoon. The action was the result of the invasion of the Franks led by Pippin, King of Italy from 781. The city had continued to grow autonomously under the local dukes, but maintained its dependence on Byzantium, with which it had close cultural and commercial ties. Venice was founded in 810, not only as a city but also as an independent state. The new descendents, who found the lagoon setting favourable for the development of political, religious and economic activities created their way of life in relation to the location and

...your houses recall the nests
of sea fowl that at times
seem attached to earth
and at times waver over water..

Cassiodorus

advantages they would obtain from it. The inhabitants established autonomous and secure centres of power and wealth on the islands in the lagoon. The 9th century saw the slow evolution of independent policies aimed at finding the necessary means of survival, culminating with the emergence of increasingly complex and systematic regulations intended for a community that, by this time, had become numerous and independent. Cittanova, Torcello, Malamocco and, finally, Rivoalto were the main seats of the first political, social and economic organisations. The decision made in 810 to transfer the seat of government to the Rialto islands was an expression of the desire to break away from a complex network of often contradictory relations and dependencies, and move towards a political and administrative structure that would benefit of the initiatives expressed individually. From the 7th century, Venetian merchants had ventured aboard their ships to more and more distant lands, going as far as the coasts of Africa. Rome could be reached by land and by sea, and intensive river traffic developed in the ports of the Adriatic and on the Italian mainland. A new socio-political order was finally set up on the islands around Rivoalto. Venice continued to expand and two important centres took shape around which the structure of the entire city developed: St. Mark's Square and the Rialto Market.

National Marciana Library. First settlements in Rialto.

Lagoon landscape.

St. Mark's Square.

Lion of St. Mark.
St. Mark's Square.

St. Mark's Square is undoubtedly the most famous example of city planning in the Serenissima, a landmark identified with the city itself. The two large areas of the square - the internal and a smaller adjoining Piazzetta that opens onto the lagoon - are defined by precise reference points:

- The church that preserves the remains of the patron saint, the Evangelist St. Mark.

- The Doges' Palace, the seat of government and of the most important courts, notably the Grand Council, the assembly of the patricians as the dominating social class. The Doge's apartments are located there, as well as space for the judicial authorities, the most important of which, after 1310, was the Council of Ten.

The Procuratie Vecchie and Nuove, the apartments of the nine most prominent magistrates of the State, the Procurators of St. Mark.

- The Procuratie Vecchie were built by the Republic towards the end of the 15th Century, in the place of a pre-existent Byzantine building; the plans by architect Mauro Coducci envisaged only the first floor over the portico of the ground floor on which another floor was added during the Renaissance. The plan and continuity of the façade, where the arches follow one another at regular intervals and without interruption, are very similar in both the Byzantine and Renaissance building.

- The Procuratie Nuove, on the opposite side of

Bridge of Sighs.

the square, were built by architect Vincenzo Scamozzi as far as the tenth archway from the Sansovinian Library. In 1582, the much earlier Orseolo Pilgrim's Hospice was demolished, leaving the Bell Tower standing alone. The architect imitated the Byzantine style and reintroduced the Sansovinian units increasing their height by one storey. The building was completed in 1640 by Baldassare Longhena.

- The square was closed on the side opposite the church by the Napoleonic Wing in neoclassic style, by the architect Giuseppe Soli. The Sansovinian church of San Geminiano was torn down, and in 1807, Napoleon ordered the construction of a grand ballroom next to the Procuratie.

- The Library that contains a priceless heritage of manuscripts and incunabula.

- The Mint, with its commercial and economic implications is where the ducat, one of the most stable European currencies, was coined.

- The Prisons, connected to the Doges'

Venice. The Arsenal.

Clock Tower.

Palace by the famous Bridge of Sighs, a covered structure suspended over the canal to serve as a link between the two buildings.

- The Bell Tower that, in every era, tolled the hours for the city and its inhabitants, was built as a defence tower during a much earlier period, under the Doge Pietro Tribuno (888-912), and was renovated many times and raised with the addition of the belfry, until it assumed its definitive appearance at the beginning of the 16th century. On 14 July 1902, it collapsed unexpectedly, but in 1912 it again stood high, *as it did and where it was.*

- The Clock Tower was built alongside the Procuratie Vecchie, between 1496 and 1499, based on plans by Codussi. The two wings were added at the beginning of the 16th Century, perhaps by the architect Pietro Lombardo. On the upper terrace the Two Moors, giant bronze jacks operated by a mechanism connected to the clock, strike the hours on the bell.

- Finally, the two columns of Mark and Theodore, brought from the Orient and set in front of the basin, symbolically guarding the city, like an immense architectural gate.

Along the north side of the Piazzetta stands the Library that was commissioned to Jacopo Sansovino by the Republic in 1532, to provide a worthy place to preserve the rare codices and manuscripts left as gifts by Petrarch and Cardinal Bessarion from as far back as 1468. In 1554, the building was completed up to the sixteenth archway beginning from the corner near the Bell Tower. Work was interrupted on the death of Sansovino and was resumed by Vincenzo Scamozzi, who completed it between 1583 and 1588, connecting it with the Mint, the façade of which is said to be the work of Ammanati.

Island of San Giorgio.

Piazzetta San Marco. Sansovinian Library.

Moscow, Pushkin Museum. Canaletto, Feast of the Sensa (detail).

Enrico Dandolo *(1192-1205)*

Planner and promoter of the Fourth Crusade (1202-1204), he took 33,500 crusaders and 4,500 horses to Constantinople. With the conquest of Constantinople he obtained immense riches in gold and works of art, like the four horses, and avenged the killing of 10,000 Venetians by the Emperor, Manuel Comnenus, in 1171. The Doge carried out the exploit at the age of 90 and his remains are preserved in the Church of Hagia Sophia in Constantinople.

Doges' Palace, Grand Council Chamber. Enrico Dandolo.

St. Mark's Basilica

According to an ancient tradition the Evangelist St. Mark passed through several islands of the lagoon during one of his numerous journeys to Aquileia. When two merchants, Tribuno da Malamocco and Rustico di Torcello, reached Venice with the body of the Evangelist, the government of the Republic decided to adopt him as patron saint in place of St. Theodore, considered too Oriental. His symbol, the winged lion, became the emblem of the city. This was the beginning of a state Church. In fact, the ecclesiastical institution of St. Mark had its own special structure, placed under the protection of the Procurators. Like the Palace, the church also underwent extensive transformations in the early centuries. Reconstruction work carried out during the dogeships of Giovanni Partecipazio (829-836), Pietro Orseolo (976-978) and Domenico Contarini (1043-1071) is well known. The last reconstruction still stands today. The plan is a Greek cross. The atrium or narthex extends around the three sides of the foot of the cross. The pilasters of the nave support the five large hemispheric domes covered with a second dome in lead. The façade of the church has two orders, the lower made up of the series of five large doorways with deep niches, the upper with five great arches and Gothic crowning. The balustrade terrace is between the two orders, with the copies of the four bronze horses in the centre (the originals are located in the Marciano Museum) brought from Constantinople after the city was conquered during the Fourth Crusade. In the interior, the narthex is marked by a series of Gothic arches that frame small blind domes entirely covered with magnificent mosaics done at the beginning of the 13th century, at the same time the church was constructed. There are illustrations of the Creation, the story of Cain and Abel, the stories of Abraham, Joseph and Moses, the construction of the Tower of Babel and other events from the Old Testament.

Marciano Museum. The four horses.

St. Mark's Basilica, narthex. Cupola, Adam and Eve.

St. Mark's Basilica. Narthex.

The large central doorway leads to the area of the church proper, which is profoundly moving. All the artistic and social developments from the mid-eleventh to the fifteenth century were included in the construction thanks to the Venetians' love for their landmark church and the skill of the artisans and carpenters who built and decorated it. The purity of the original space is astonishing, as are the Gothic-Romanesque interventions, columns, capitals, and balustrades; the rare marble brought from the Orient with great difficulty, set like gems and recreated in the new setting; the magnificent mosaic surfaces where the gold of the background conveys a surreal aura that seems to allude to a spiritual and almost magical world. The chancel is divided from the nave by an elaborate iconostasis done in the Gothic style, with statues of the Virgin, St. John the Evangelist and the Twelve Apostles by Delle Masegne, set above the architrave. The **Gold Altarpiece** stands

out behind the main altar. Of inestimable value, work continued on it for many years until it finally took on its current and definitive appearance in the 14th century. The mosaic composition on the walls and vaults, begun under Doge Domenico Selvo (1071-1084) and, of which small fragments remain, was continued and developed in the 12th and 13th centuries. The mosaics cover an area of about 4,000 sq. m. and some parts were restored well beyond the 16th century.

The church is built on three levels, a path symbolising different levels of sacredness that reaches its climax in the chancel. To the right of the chancel is the doge's throne. The main altar is bordered by a balustrade with statues of the four evangelists, the work of Jacopo Sansovino, and it preserves the sarcophagus holding the body of St. Mark. The chancel is set apart and serves as the Palatine Chapel, in direct communication with the Doges' Palace. The floor (12th century) is of great interest. The Iconostasis (1394), the marble curtain that separates the chancel, is the work of Jacobello and Pierpaolo delle Masegne. The door of the sacristy with bas-reliefs of the Resurrection and the Descent from the Cross is a masterpiece by Jacopo Sansovino. The Marciano Museum was set up in the rooms where the mosaicists of the basilica used to work. The doge's throne and Flemish tapestries of the 15th and 16th centuries are noteworthy. The

St. Mark's. South Transept.

Gold altarpiece. Archangel Michael.

Chancel, ciborium and the gold altarpiece.

St. Mark's

Great Arches and Domes

In the lunette, Christ the Pantocrator dominates the throne. The mosaics belong to various periods: from the 12th-13th on, up to the 18th Cent.

ST. MARK'S

DOMES OF THE PENTECOST AND THE ASCENSION

Dome of the Pentecost. *The mosaics can be dated to the first half of the 12th Cent. The divine spirit descends over the heads of the Apostles in the form of tongues of fire. The figures between the windows represent the various countries where the Apostles preached the Gospel.*

Dome of the Ascension. *The mosaics are from the first half of the 13th Cent. Christ is lifted up towards infinity by four angels below, the Virgin between two angels and the Twelve Apostles can be seen. Further down between the windows are representations of virtues and beatitudes.*

Jacobello and Pierpaolo delle Masegne, Iconostasis.

Column with reliefs (partial view).

St. Mark's Basilica. Nave.

name of the Horses, given to the external loggia of the façade, goes back to the 13th century when the horses brought from Constantinople were placed there. Today the loggia holds copies of the originals, kept in the museum. The Zen Chapel was located in the south-west corner of the transept from 1504-21 for the tomb of Cardinal Giambattista Zen. The baptistery was placed in the south wing of the narthex in the 14th century, during the period of Doge Andrea Dandolo (1342-54). The treasure of St. Mark, rich with ancient and rare relics, is located in three rooms: the Ante-Treasury, Sanctuary and Treasury.

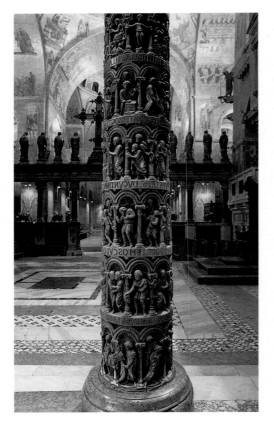

DOGES' PALACE

POLITICAL CENTRE

The Doges' Palace of Venice contains three styles in exactly the same proportion: Romanesque, Gothic and Arab. It is the central construction of the world.

Ruskin, The Stones of Venice.

The Doges' Palace in Venice dates from the beginning of the 9th century (810), when the government transferred its seat from Malamocco to Rivoalto. In the beginning, it is likely that some of the existing buildings belonging to Doge Angelo Partecipazio were used. The ideal reconstruction of the first building coincides with a purely defensive building with a nearly square plan, surrounded by high walls and corner towers. With the rise of Venetian power and peaceful domestic politics, the Palace assumed more open forms, porticos and loggias; this was

Pietro Gradenigo *(1289 -1311)*

In 1297, he brought about one of the most important events of constitutional politics, know as the 'Serrata del Maggior Consiglio': the doge, who was not favoured by the population, succeeded in concentrating power in the hands of the patrician families and decided the method for electing the members. Only those who had participated in the sessions of the Grand Council during the previous four years could be elected to attend. From then on the government became an oligarchy.

Doges' Palace, Grand Council Chamber. Pietro Gradenigo.

(p.27) Doges' Palace, west façade, partial view.

South-west corner. Adam and Eve.

West façade. Justice

the period of Doge Sebastiano Ziani (1172-78). By end of the 12th century, the need arose for a radical transformation to accommodate the highest magistracy, the Grand Council, whose task was to make laws and elect all the other magistracies including the doge. Work began in 1340 with the renovation of the wing facing the basin. The old towers disappeared and the Byzantine edifice was demolished in favour of the new building, from the canal to the Piazzetta. The quatrefoiled loggia extends over the ground floor portico. It is on

this structure of columns and arches that the voluminous space of the Grand Council stands. Its wall is pierced with large ogival windows, and it is also lightened thanks to the two-coloured marble flooring, with alternating white Istrian stone and rose marble from Verona.

In 1424, under Doge Francesco Foscari (1423-1457), construction of the building near the Piazzetta began, done in the same Gothic style as the existing buiding in order to respect the structural and stylistic continuity demanded by the gov-

Corner, Porta della Carta. Solomon's Judgement.

ernment. The fourteenth-century building (1438-1443) extends to the Palace entrance: the Gothic Porta della Carta, by Giovanni and Bartolomeo Bon.

After passing through the doorway and continuing along the passage dominated by the arches of the Foscari Arch one reaches the Giants' Stairway, a Renaissance work by Antonio Rizzo, who also planned the reconstruction of the eastern wing of the Palace facing the canal, following a terrible fire that destroyed the doge's apartments in 1483.

This edifice, which begins at the apsidal area of St. Mark's Church and joins the fourteenth-century building near the basin, was only completed in the middle of the 16th century. The doges' apartments were located here up to the first floor; the College Hall, Senate Chamber and the meeting-chamber of the Council of Ten were in the second section of the building. Pietro Lombardo and then Scarpagnino continued the work of Rizzo, following the original plans. During the doge-

Doges' Palace, west façade.

Francesco Foscari *(1423-1457).*

He was the doge who urged Venice to expand on the mainland, a policy that, as Tommaso Mocenigo said, "will make you poorer, and of two houses you will remain with only one". In the thirty-year rule of Doge Foscari, Venice acquired power, but lost trade. In 1454, Mohammed II conquered Constantinople. Foscari was deposed and died in his palazzo on the Grand Canal while the bells rang for the election of the new doge.

Doges' Palace, Grand Council Chamber. Francesco Foscari.

ship of Andrea Gritti (1523-39), the architect Jacopo Sansovino added the Golden Stairway in the main part of the building and it became the courtly passageway from the loggia to the floor of the great halls and to the doge's apartments.

Most of the decorations were renovated after the fire in 1573 which destroyed important works. In the Room of the Anticollegio there are four paintings by Tintoretto portraying mythological scenes: *Mercury and the Graces*, *Vulcan's Forge*, *Minerva repelling Mars*, and *Ariadne, Venus and Bacchus*. On the wall in front of the window, the painting on the left is Paolo Veronese's *The Rape of Europa*; the one on the right is, *The Return of Jacob* by Jacopo Bassano. The internal

Grand Council Chamber.

Grand Council Chamber. Paolo Veronese, The Apotheosis of Venice (details).

decoration of the rooms as well as the design of the ceilings and fireplaces was carried out according to the plans of Andrea Palladio, Vincenzo Scamozzi and Cristoforo Sorte, initially by Giovanni Antonio Rusconi and later by Antonio da Ponte, the palace overseer. The ceiling of the College Hall is rich and elegant. Carved golden frames hold the wonderful paintings by Paolo Veronese and portray the Virtues along the sides; in the centre: *Mars and Neptune, Faith* and *Venice between Justice and Peace*. All are allegories praising Justice and the land and sea power of Venice. On the walls, in addition to the painting by Veronese above the throne portraying *The Allegory of the Battle of Lepanto*, there are paintings by Tintoretto, on com-

memorative subjects of several doges such as Da Ponte and Gritti. The painting in the centre, *The Triumphal exaltation of Venice at sea* is also by Jacopo Tintoretto. The Senate Chamber was also called the Pregadi. In 1577, a second great fire destroyed the Ballot Room and the Grand Council Chamber. On the wall towards the Basin there are stories showing the Fourth Crusade in 1204; the one near the courtyard portrays the dispute between Frederick Barbarossa and Pope Alexander III. In the centre, Jacopo Tintoretto, who did the painting above the throne portraying *Paradise*; also painted *Venice the Queen*. Veronese was commissioned to do *The Apotheosis of Venice* whereas Palma il Giovane painted the others.

GRAND CANAL

THE ROUTE OF THE NOBLES

The Grand Canal, called Canalazzo by the Venetians, is the waterway that crosses the city forming wide moderate bends, revealing its river origins amidst the deep waters of the lagoon. It is crossed by four bridges: the Accademia, the Scalzi, the Calatrava and the Rialto.

Palazzi. Palazzo Corner della Ca' Grande was built by Jacopo Corner between 1532 and 1561 and was designed by Jacopo Sansovino. The School and Monastery of Santa Maria della Carità now houses the Academy of Fine Arts; Palazzo Giustinian-Lolin was, one of the first works of Longhena. Palazzo Rezzonico with its immense ballroom and monumental stairway is now the Museum of Eighteenth-century Venetian Art. The Palazzi Giustin-

ian and Foscari, the latter of the doge, house the University of Venice: they were designed by Giovanni and Bartolomeo Bon. Palazzo Balbi was built between 1582 and 1590 by Alessandro Vittoria. Palazzo Grassi. Palazzi Mocenigo. Palazzo Grimani by Michele Sanmicheli built during the first half of the 16th century. Palazzo Coccina Tiepolo by Guglielmo dei Grigi, the Byzantine Palazzi Farsetti-Dandolo and Loredan Corner dating from the twelfth-thirteenth century. Palazzo dei Camerlenghi by Guglielmo dei Grigi, built between 1525 and 1528; Fontego dei Tedeschi, Ca' da Mosto, Ca' d'Oro, Gothic from the second half of the 15th century. Palazzo Pesaro, a building by Baldassare Longhena and Palazzo Vendramin Calergi by architect Mauro Coducci.

Basilica of Santa Maria della Salute.

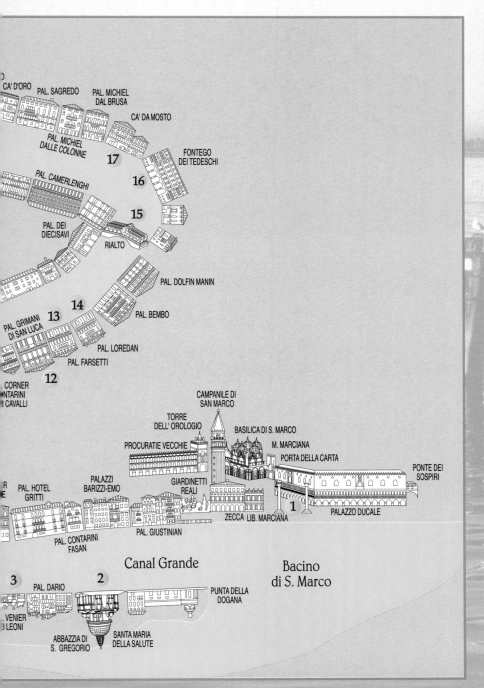

Church of Saints John and Paul (SS. Giovanni e Paolo).

Andrea Verrocchio. Equestrian statue of Bartolomeo Colleoni.

Church of Saints John and Paul. In the Castello district, near the new edge of the lagoon, there is a very important and inspiring group of buildings located around the Campo SS. Giovanni e Paolo, with the church of the same name, the Scuola Grande di San Marco, the Mendicants' Hospice along the adjoining fondamenta and, in the centre of the spacious campo, the equestrian statue portraying Bartolomeo Colleoni. The construction of the church took two centuries and it was finally consecrated in 1430. The interior has a nave and two aisles in an Egyptian-cross layout with five apsidal chapels. The church ranks immediately after St. Mark's in importance. The doges and other illustrious figures were buried here. The adjoining Scuola Grande was begun by the architect Pietro Lombardo in 1487 and continued by Mauro Coducci. The statue of Colleoni cast by Andrea Verrocchio was put up in 1488.

Chiesa di Santa Maria dei Frari. The Church of Santa Maria Gloriosa dei Frari - also known as the Friars' Church - is another important church built in the Gothic style between the 14th and 15th century. Begun in 1340 with the nucleus of the apsidal structure, it was completed in 1443, though it was not consecrated until 1469. The result in the interior is grand with a nave and two aisles divided by 12 robust columns that support the high ogival cross-vault ceiling. The transept is even more spa-

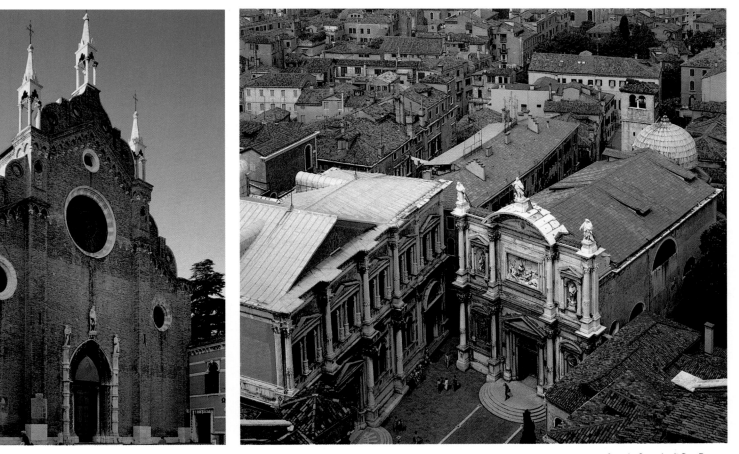

Chiesa di Santa Maria Gloriosa dei Frari.

Scuola Grande di San Rocco.

cious with aligned apses that stand out clearly. At the point where the nave intersects the transept, the church - the only one in Venice to do so - has maintained the wooden choir with rare carved stalls in three orders, a work done by Marco Cozzi in 1468. There are important Gothic and Renaissance funeral monuments along the walls of the church. The central chapel contains the masterpiece *The Assumption*, which Titian painted in 1518. The works *Virgin with Infant Jesus* and *Musician angels* by Giovanni Bellini (1482) are displayed in the sacristy. There is also the wooden sculpture painted by Donatello portraying a care-worn *St. John the Baptist* and the equally famous *Pesaro Altarpiece*, also by Titian.

Scuola Grande di San Rocco. Construction began in 1515 and continued for more than fifty years. Bartolomeo Bon, who supervised work up to the first order, was succeeded by Scarpagnino and Giangiacomo dei Grigi. Tintoretto did one of his most im-

Church of the Frari.
G. Bellini, musician angel.

portant series of works for this school between 1564 and 1588. Eight paintings with scenes from the New Testament, including *The Flight to Egypt*, hang on the walls of the ground-floor room. There are 23 paintings by Tintoretto, commissioned by the School, in the room on the first floor. The artist completed those on the ceiling by 1578 and those on the walls by 1581. The subjects of the paintings on the ceiling are episodes from the Old Testament, while those on the walls treat episodes from the New Testament. Tintoretto did the work in a very short time and they were completed by 1581. The ceiling, divided into sections, shows *Saint Roch in Glory* in the centre and the other panels portray allegoric figures of the Great Schools of Venice and figures of cherubs and virtues. The signed Crucifixion on the wall dates from 1565. Other paintings show episodes of Christ's martyrdom. The two paintings portraying Christ carrying the cross and the dead Christ are by Titian.

Giotto (1267-1337)

"Giotto changed the art of painting from Greek to Latin, and made it modern".
This is what Cennini said at the end of the 14ᵗʰ Century, putting into focus, with
good critical intuition, the meaning of the renewal introduced by the Florentine
artist in painting. Giotto was able to go beyond the expressive lightness of Byzantine
art by introducing nature and history into painting.

Giotto, Scrovegni Chapel. Noli me tangere (detail).

PADUA

Just a half-hour drive from Venice, Padua is one of the most visited cities in the Veneto, and it has been an important spiritual, cultural and artistic centre since the Middle Ages. For many, Padua is above all the city of Saint Anthony, who lived here for several years, and died here in 1237. The following year, his numerous devotees and followers began work on the construction of an imposing basilica where his body lies. Externally, the edifice is characterised by a cross-section of styles, in particular Lombard, Tuscan and Byzantine, and is surmounted by 8 Oriental-style domes. The spacious and solemn interior follows the form of the Latin cross with a nave and two aisles, separated by large pilasters. Works of art of inestimable value are preserved here: sculptures of Donatello, frescoes by Giusto de' Menabuoi and Altichiero da Zevio (late 14ᵗʰ century). The equestrian statue of Gattamelata, done by Donatello in 1453, rises nobly in the parvis.

Prato della Valle is an example of the Veneto garden re-proposed in neoclassical style. It is an immense ellipsoid shaped area encircled by ancient dwellings and by the Church of Saint Justine.

Via Belludi and the Basilica of Saint Anthony.

Prato della Valle.

Basilica of Saint Anthony. Apse.

Scrovegni Chapel. Giotto, an Evangelist.

Basilica of Saint Anthony, parvis. Donatello, equestrian statue of Gattamelata.

The **University** of Padua was founded in 1222. Of the old complex, including the six-teenth-century Palazzo Bo, there remain the internal courtyard, the Anatomy theatre (late 16th century), the Aula Magna, and the Sala dei Quaranta, with Galileo's chair.

The **Caffè Pedrocchi**, inaugurated in 1831, was designed for Antonio Pedrocchi by Giuseppe Jappelli.

The **Scrovegni Chapel.** It took Giotto on-ly three years, from 1303 to 1306, to com-plete the series of frescoes in the Scrovegni Chapel in which he recounts the life of Mary's parents Joachim and Anne, the life of the Virgin and episodes of the life and death of Christ.

Palladio and the Venetian Villas. Padua and Venice are connected by the Brenta canal. Dotting its bank are many aristocratic villas and country residences of Venetian nobles, designed by the masterly hand of Andrea Palladio, who was born in Padua in 1508. The most beautiful and well known are Villa Pisani in Strà, Villa Foscari, com-monly known as the Malcontenta, and Villa Cornaro in Piombino Dese, built between 1552 and 1570 by the Venetian architect for the offspring of a rich Venetian family.

House and statue of Juliet.

Arena, partial external view.

VERONA

Shakespeare wrote the tragedy, Romeo and Juliet, drawing from the events of two families from Verona, the Montagues from which Romeo came, and the Capulets to which Juliet belonged (moved by a spirit of love and hate). The two protagonists fell in love at first sight, but when their families met, they turned quickly from offensive remarks to violence and one of them fell wounded and died. This led to the desire for revenge. The two lovers fell more deeply in love each time they met, and though they suffered from the effects of the hatred that divided their families, they tried to find a way to unite in marriage. The relationship between Romeo and Juliet is distinguished by fascinating thoughts *"...see how she lays her cheek upon her hand!"* Romeo (Act 2, Scene 2); *"My bounty is as boundless as the sea, My love as deep; the more I give to thee, The more I have, for both are infinite"!* (Act 2, Scene 2); Juliet *"...leap to these arms, untalk'd of and unseen. / Lovers can see to do their amorous rites by their own beauties; or if love be blind, it best agrees with night..."* (Act 3, Scene 2); *"come gentle night, come, loving black-brow'd night, give me my Romeo"* (Act 3, Scene 2). But Juliet was distressed by the departure of Romeo - *"Methinks I see thee, now thou art below, as one dead in the bottom of a tomb"* (Act 3, Scene 5); *"Romeo, I come, this do I drink to thee"!* (Act 4, Scene 3) - and ultimately killed her-

Roman theatre and the Pietra Bridge.

self. The conclusion of the tragedy of Romeo and Juliet did not lead to the catharsis of hatred, and although the two families erected golden monuments to the two lovers, hatred -like love - continues to stir the hearts of mankind.

Verona is also a city that offers the visitor important sights. The **Arena** is the most famous monument, but there is also the Museum of Castelvecchio and the churches. Visistors can also enjoy a stroll through the town centre, to **Piazza Bra** that connects the area of the Roman Forum. **Lake Garda**, surrounded by hills covered with vineyards and olive groves, is just a short distance away.

Castelvecchio. Equestrian statue
of Cangrande della Scala.

View of Verona with the
Castelvecchio Bridge and the Arena.

Florence

The city of Florence stands out for its art and culture. As early as the end of the 13th Century, Florence moved away from medieval civilisation with the work of Cimabue and Giotto, who drew a new human figure in the frescoes and paintings of the saints. Dante, Petrarch and Boccaccio transformed religious principles and human passions into poetry.

During the 15th Century the Medici family: Cosimo the Elder and Lorenzo the Magnificent, the most famous, amidst the whirl

Florence, a view.

of unrestrainable power struggles, brought together the culture of the previous centuries in their palazzo in Via Larga, sending emissaries to Europe, Greece and Asia Minor to gather codices and parchments, and to attract scholars in the Arts and Sciences. Open to the opinions of artists and learned men with whom he knew how to surround himself, and in particular defended by the support of the anti-pope John XXIII, Cosimo decided to transfer to Florence the Council for the Reunification of Churches, whose council fathers from Basel had stopped in Ferrara. To move such a large group of people, some of whom in ripe old age, including horses, means of transport, and the mass of servants to carry out various mansions, had increased costs beyond measure. Cosimo attempted to interest and attract Florentines, so that they would contribute their share. More than the refusal he received, he was saddened by the narrow-mindedness of his fellow citizens, incapable of foreseeing the advantages that would have followed for the city. The Cathedral and the convent of Santa Maria Novella were the areas set aside for meetings; Palazzo Medici in Via Larga, newly built by Michelozzo, and the streets where the population gathered to get a glimpse of these figures from such a different world, were the places where the city's two social class, the middle class and the common people, met. The result of this unique situation was a high degree of development.

The Guilds – this was the name given to the associations that governed public goods – continued to announce competitions to assign work to be done, such as the dome of Santa Maria del Fiore that, due to its sheer size, represented a difficult problem to resolve, and the decoration of the doors of the Baptistery. The population took part in the fervent activity in the workshops and in the streets, speaking with

Sansepolcro, Civic Museum.
Piero della Francesca,
Polyptych of the Misericordia (detail).

masters and assistants and showing a lively interest in public life.

One could meet Brunelleschi, Lorenzo Ghiberti occupied adding and removing the panels of the East Door of the Baptistery, Masaccio (1401-1428) working on the Brancacci Chapel of the Church of Santa Maria del Carmine, Donatello who was creating the statue of St. George and the one of David, the first figure of a nude in the Renaissance. And of course, Botticelli, (1444/5-1510), whose paintings recall the period of Lorenzo the Magnificent, Michelangelo, Leonardo da Vinci, and Raphael.

Europe was born in 15th Century Florence.
The Splendour of Italy presents Florence in the 15th and 16th Centuries, its streets and its museums, the unparalleled Uffizi, where the inhabitants, even if in a different manner, continue to hold high their past.

Palazzo Medici-Riccardi, chapel.
Benozzo Gozzoli, Journey of the Magi to Bethlehem

Sansepolcro, Civic Museum.
Piero della Francesca, Resurrection.

Palazzo Vecchio, the Hall of the 500
Michelangelo, The Genius of Victory.

Piazza della Signoria.
Palazzo Vecchio, cornice
above the entrance door.

Arringhiera. Donatello,
Judith and Holofernes (copy).

Badia Church. Bell tower.

Palazzo della Signoria.

PIAZZA DELLA SIGNORIA

The square is bounded by Palazzo della Signoria, the Loggia dei Lanzi, the Tribunale di Mercanzia and Palazzo Uguccioni and it is adorned by the fountain in the square and by the equestrian statue of Cosimo I. Palazzo della Signoria, or Palazzo Vecchio, complete with battlements, was built with stone blocks that give it a massive architectural style. It is the building in which the age-old struggle for power took place and government decisions were reached. Leaving Piazza della Signoria, along Via dei Calzaioli, one arrives at the group composed of the Basilica of Santa Maria del Fiore, the Baptistery and Giotto's Bell tower. This group of political and religious buildings was designed by Arnolfo di Cambio, and each one reflects distinct characteristics that marked the direction in which Florentine architecture developed.

Loggia della Signoria.
Benvenuto Cellini, statue of Perseus.

Loggia della Signoria.
Giambologna, The Rape of the Sabines (detail).

Piazza della Signoria.
Fountain of Neptune and monument to Cosimo I.

The **fountain of the piazza** was designed by Ammanati who built it with his assistants between 1563 and 1575. The statue of Neptune, god of the sea, in white marble, dominates the bronze ones of the Nereids, reclining on the edges of the basin. The work is in the Baroque style.

The **equestrian statue of Cosimo**, first Duke of Florence (1537-1574), is also famous for the fact that several episodes in the duke's life are carved in the pedestal. In one, the seventeen-year-old duke can be admired in a remissive pose, while he asks the senators to be recognised as head of the city. The statue was designed and cast by Giambologna in 1594 and describes that particular event.

The **Loggia** was a peculiar building that rose among the dwellings of the consorts, opening onto the street, where commemorations and official meetings were held. It was a remarkable building because of the importance of its architecture and

the works of art that were displayed there: architecture and sculpture increased the prestige of those associated with it. There were many loggias in Florence in the 14th and 15th centuries, and the Loggia della Signoria was the most striking example. During the period of the Grand Duchy, the Loggia della Signoria was used as the guardroom of the Lansquenets, the Grand Duke's special guard. Today, several ancient statues are displayed, such as the lion in Greek marble and two

sculptures by Giambologna: Hercules and the centaur Nessus, and the Rape of the Sabines. Perseus (1553), the bronze masterpiece by Benvenuto Cellini, can also be seen here. Art during this period followed the parameters of beauty set by the works of Michelangelo, Leonardo da Vinci and Raphael. Cellini did this work in the style of Michelangelo, dominating the elements with remarkable work in goldsmithery that gives the surface a splendid luminosity.

ART

Ponte Vecchio.

Uffizi Gallery. Titian, The Urbino Venus.

Towards the end of the 13th century, after the sculptures of Nicola Pisano and the paintings of Cimabue, the works of two famous artists appeared: Arnolfo, architect and sculptor, and Giotto, painter and sculptor. It could be said that they established a school of art stimulated by Florence's intense trade with the cities of the peninsula and with countries beyond the Alps. Giotto was active in Florence, Assisi, Rome and Padua and had a large group of followers, commonly called "Giotteschi", including Taddeo Gaddi, Bernardo Daddi and Maso di Banco. Arnolfo di Cambio, well known for his architecture and sculpture, was also summoned to work at the Papal Court. In the 14th century, artists grew in number in Florence and included Nardo di Cione, Andrea Bonaiuti, Giottino, Giovanni da Milano, Spinello Aretino, Agnolo Gaddi, Starnina, Gerini and the Bicci. These painters followed the styles and influences of artistic movements from various countries. Gentile da Fabriano, whose pictorial delicacy was seen as superior to the others, resumed the international Gothic style. At the beginning of the 15th century, this school of painting established itself for its sharper and more incisive features. Masaccio is representative of the art of this period: in spite of his short life (he died in 1428 at just 27 years of age), he placed man and nature at the centre of his interests. The figures and the landscapes in which they move are mixed with a dense colour, rendering them participants in human nature. It was towards the end of the 15th century that painting produced high-quality works that would rarely be matched in later centuries. The artwork in Florence during this period was closely connected to the Medici family and to religious communities. Painters, sculptors and architects were active in various parts of the city, in the churches and monasteries. The best known names are Filippo Lippi, Fra Angelico, Paolo Uccello, Andrea del Castagno, Domenico Veneziano, Alessio Baldovinetti, il Pesellino, Antonio del Pollaiuolo and Andrea del Verrocchio. In architecture: Brunelleschi, Cronaca, Giuliano da Sangallo, Antonio da Sangallo, and Leon Battista Alberti. In sculpture: Cellini, Bartolomeo Ammanati, Vasari and many others. The eminent painter Sandro Botticelli uniquely rendered the atmosphere of the period of Lorenzo de' Medici. Fra Angelico, Domenico Ghirlandaio and Filippino Lippi also worked during this period. Michelangelo, Leonardo da Vinci and Raphael were the artists who, between the 15th and 16th centuries brought architecture, sculpture and painting to their highest and unequalled pinnacle. In the paintings of Leonardo at the Uffizi, and in the Mona Lisa at the Louvre, sfumatos accomplish the task of spiritual penetration in the image. Raphael identified his art with a refined sense of religiousness, stemming from the softness of the colours and poses of the figures. They were followed by Fra' Bartolomeo, Ridolfo del Ghirlandaio, Andrea del Sarto, Franciabigio, Pontormo, and Rosso Fiorentino. Though the Renaissance is over, the fame of Florentine art continues to be a pole of attraction throughout the world.

Bargello National Museum. Donatello, David.

Basilica Santa Maria del Fiore. Domenico di Michelino, Dante with the Divine Comedy.

*Uffizi Gallery.
Sandro Botticelli, Birth of Venus.*

Arnolfo di Cambio *(1232-1302).*

Architecture and sculpture were the expressions of his artistic activity. His most significant works include the plans for Palazzo Vecchio and the Cathedral of Santa Maria del Fiore. The document with which the Seigniory commissioned him to build Palazzo Vecchio also contained the following concept: "... may a fortress be built so as to preserve the Supreme Council of the citizens from their own turbulent party spirit".

Cathedral Museum.
Arnolfo di Cambio, statue of Pope Boniface VIII.

PALAZZO VECCHIO (OR DELLA SIGNORIA)

Arnolfo di Cambio planned the construction of Palazzo Vecchio in 1298, and despite additions during the following centuries, the original layout has been preserved. Towers and walls of granite blocks, cornices along each storey, and unreachable narrow double lancet windows give the square-shaped building, with its crowning and towers, the appearance of a fortress. The building became the residence of the Gonfalonier and the Priors, members of the Seigniory.

The Arringhiera, a platform on which the Seigniory would sit during ceremonial occasions, was built outside adjacent to the doorway. Several statues are still displayed, most of which are copies: the statue of Marzocco, the crouching lion that symbolised the city's power (enemies were forced to kiss its thighs); the group of Judith and Holofernes, the symbol of justice sculpted by Donatello for a fountain in Palazzo Medici and transported here in 1493 after the family was expelled from Florence; Michelangelo's David recalling the enthusiasm with which the citizenry accompanied the statue from the workshop (the 1504 original is in the Academy Gallery). The courtyard expresses the style of Michelozzo, architect of Cosimo the Elder.

The winged genius on the fountain is by Verrocchio (1476) and the original is inside. The stuccowork on the pillars and the frescoes with

Palazzo Vecchio. Study of Francesco de' Medici (detail).

views of property of the House of Austria were done in 1576. The armoury, a room with pilasters and cross vaults, belongs to the original building. The great staircase (1560-1563) leads to the Hall of the 500. The room, impressive in size, was planned in 1495 by Simone del Pollaiuolo, nicknamed "Il Cronaca" to accommodate meetings of the five hundred representatives of the population. Notable events that took place include the terrifying sermons of Girolamo Savonarola and the sentence that condemned him to be hanged and burnt. The Genius of Victory by Michelangelo, one of the works that should have embellished the tomb of Pope Julius II is an example of the plastic arts, while the paintings on the ceiling and walls by Vasari and his assistants belong to the pictorial arts. The numerous remaining rooms in the palazzo are adorned with

Palazzo Vecchio. Study of Francesco de' Medici.

Palazzo Vecchio. The courtyard.

Palazzo Vecchio. The Lily chamber.

paintings and carved gilt ceilings capable of awakening interest in a tradition of historical importance. They are the rooms of the Otto di Pratica, the Duecento; and those that make up the Monumental Quarters and the Quarters of the Elements. The apartment of Eleanor of Toledo, wife of Duke Cosimo I, is composed of six rooms, two halls, and two chapels: the Green Room, Eleanor's chapel, the Room of the Sabines and the reception room; the rooms of Esther, Penelope, and Gualdrada. The chapel of the Seigniory, the Audience Chamber and the Lily Chamber follow, and, finally the chancellery and the cloak-room.

Palazzo degli Uffizi. Courtyard.

Palazzo degli Uffizi.

The Palazzo degli Uffizi is a building with two wings that extend from *Via della Ninna* and from the *Loggia dei Lanzi* towards the *Arno River*; on the side where the two wings meet, high arches on the ground floor provide light and air to the courtyard. The statues of famous personalities are displayed in the niches along the internal façade. Inside the corridors and in the rooms on the top floor, the artwork forming the Uffizi Gallery can be admired.

Uffizi Gallery. Sandro Botticelli, Spring.

UFFIZI GALLERY

*Uffizi Gallery
Hugo van der Goes, Portinari triptych
Maria Portinari and daughter.*

The **Uffizi Gallery** is one of the best-known collections of artwork, paintings and sculptures. Its origin goes back to the artistic tradition of the Medici family. Cosimo the Elder and Lorenzo the Magnificent laid the foundation of this collection that would later inspire and increase the enthusiasm for the fine arts among the citizenry of Florence. The Medici Popes, Leo X and Clement VII and the Grand Dukes contributed greatly ending with the provisions of the 18th century that bequeathed the collection of the Uffizi to the city of Florence.

Statues include *The Sleeping Hermaphrodite* (2nd century B.C.), *The Medici Venus*, a copy of an original by Praxiteles (3rd century B.C.); *The Knife-whetter*, replica of an original (3rd century B.C.) by the school of Pergamum; and *The Wrestlers*, *The Faun*, *The Little Apollo*, copies of Greek statues. The group of Niobe and children is a later work of Scopas and is displayed in a late-eighteenth-century setting.

The **paintings** are gathered together in three sections: the first one features early Florentine and Sienese works; the second has fifteenth-century works by the Venetian, Emilia, German and Flemish schools; the third one has masterpieces (16th-18th centuries) by the Flemish and French schools.

Cimabue, Madonna di Santa Trìnita, and on the side Giotto, Madonna enthroned and angels. Paintings by the Sienese school: Duccio di Boninsegna, the Rucellai Madonna (13th –14th century); Simone Martini and Lippo Memmi, Annunciation. The dialogue between the Angel and the Virgin Mary is expressed by the movement of a sinuous line as if to underscore the words that vibrate in the air. Gentile da Fabriano, Adoration of the Magi; Fra Angelico, Coronation of the Virgin; Masaccio, Madonna. The line of development of Florentine painting proceeds from Giotto to Masaccio. Paolo Uccello, the Battle of San Romano: one of the examples of the research in perspective of the great master. Piero della Francesca, the portraits of Frederick of Montefeltro and Battista Sforza, are filled with spirituality. Alessio Baldovinetti, Annunciation; Filippo Lippi, Coronation of the Virgin (1447). Benozzo Gozzoli portrayed life in fifteenth-century Florence.

Sandro Botticelli *(1444/5-1510)*

He was a pupil of Filippo Lippi and Verrocchio. His works include The Fortress, Madonna of the Pomegranate and Madonna of the Magnificat and close to the atmosphere and life in the palazzo and garden of the Medici, are his masterpieces: The Birth of Venus and the Spring.

Sandro Botticelli, Adoration of the Magi. Self-portrait.

Spring (1476-78) and the *The Birth of Venus* (1482) by Sandro Botticelli are particularly inspiring paintings, capable of captivating the onlooker's attention for the atmosphere they emanate. The lightness of the figures, the presence of nature and the transparency of the water and sky are a result of the light lines, devoid of a minimal sense of materiality. In the *Adora-* *tion of the Magi* the Medici are portrayed in acts of devotion, even though they appear to be gathered in a family reunion in the presence of the painter. Hugo Van der Goes, the *Portinari triptych*; Leonardo da Vinci, *Adoration of the Magi*, an exquisite sketch and the *Annunciation*, a work of the Florentine period. Andrea del Verrocchio, master of Leonardo, *Baptism of*

Simone Martini, Annunciation (detail).

Leonardo da Vinci, Adoration of the Magi

Sandro Botticelli, the Birth of Venus (detail).

Christ. The Tribune (Buontalenti, 1580-88). The atmosphere of the setting that the architect succeeded in creating should be noted. Luca Signorelli, *The Holy Family*. The work of Michelangelo draws on these nudes. Dürer, *Adoration of the Magi* (1504), and works of Lucas Cranach, Albert Altdorfer, Holbein the Younger. Giovanni Bellini, *Adoration of the Magi, Circumcision*, Andrea Mantegna, *Ascension*. Flemish and German masters. Correggio, *The Rest on the Flight into Egypt*. Michelangelo, *Holy Family*, a rare easel work; the contrast between the Christian and pagan world, force and movement of the composition are evident. Raphael painted Pope Leo X with the Cardinals Luigi de' Rossi and Giulio de' Medici, the future Pope Clement VII. The colours and indefinite lines create a perfect balance in this courtly

Giovanni de' Medici

Sandro Botticelli

Lorenzo the Magnificent   *Cosimo the Elder*   *Piero the Gouty*   *Giuliano de' Medici*

scene in which the pope is portrayed seated, surrounded by prelates, in a fixed and concentrated pose. It seems as if the scene was done during the pause from a heated discussion. The echo of the words that have been uttered remains in the room, moving through the air and suffocating the restricted space. Threats and passion are the concepts that this painting emanates. Paolo Veronese, *Holy Family, Martyrdom of Saint Justine*. Tintoretto, *Portrait of Ja-*

copo Sansovino. Leandro Bassano, *Family Concert*, Jacopo Bassano *Portrait of an artist*. Peter Paul Rubens, *Portrait of Isabella Brandt*; Anthony Van Dyck, portraits.

The revolution of Angelo Merisi, nicknamed Caravaggio, after his birthplace, led to the end of Mannerism. The artist broke with the tradition of contemporary artists through a particular use of light and the portrayal of scenes of crude reality. This is evident in the paintings of the Medusa, the adolescent Bacchus and his portrayal of the sacrifice of Isaac. The *Medusa* is the enraged head of a woman with a wild look in her eyes, her hair a mass of cruel snakes and blood spurting from her severed head.

The head of Bacchus is very exotic. The young man is presented as the image of pleasure, savouring the infinite ways of sensuality and perversion. His large eyes are dominated by thick prominent eyebrows,

puffy lips and a pinkish complexion. He appears to continue savouring pleasure as he recalls it. This work is followed by several portraits by Rembrandt Van Rijn. Painting of the 17th and 18th centuries is represented by the works of Mattia Preti, Giovanni Lys, Domenico Fetti, and Strozzi. Paintings of Reni and the Carracci are also displayed, while the Venetian school is present with paintings by G. B. Piazzetta, Pietro Longhi, G. B. Tiepolo, Canaletto and Francesco Guardi.

Sandro Botticelli, Adoration of the Magi.

Michelangelo, Holy Family.

Filippo Brunelleschi (1377-1446)

The competition for the decoration of the doors of the Baptistery won by Lorenzo Ghiberti, prompted the artist to move to Rome to study the dome of the Pantheon. When he returned to Florence he undertook the construction of the dome of Santa Maria del Fiore, but refused to reveal the procedure he would use. He was assigned the project despite the tenacity with which he guarded his secret.

Church of Santa Maria del Carmine, Brancacci chapel
Masaccio, portrait of Filippo Brunelleschi.

BASILICA OF SANTA MARIA DEL FIORE

Florence. Basilica of Santa Maria del Fiore. Interior.

The French writer André Suares defined the bell tower as the fantasy of Florence, the caprice of a city in which beauty is calculated, reason seeks all rules, and poetry cedes to the rigour of the line. It escapes the art of building and has the fascination of an illusion and of the imagination...

Florence. Giotto's bell tower
Brunelleschi's dome
Façade of the Basilica of Santa Maria del Fiore
and the roof of the Baptistery.

The first church built in this area in the 11th century was dedicated to Santa Reparata. At the end of the 13th century the government commissioned Arnolfo di Cambio to build a new church. When the plan was completed, Arnolfo began construction; after his death work passed to Giotto, Talenti and to Brunelleschi. The Basilica of Santa Maria del Fiore, so called because of the fleur-de-lys emblem of Florence, was planned by Arnolfo di Cambio in 1296 and finished in 1436 with the completion of the dome designed by Brunelleschi. The façade is from the 19th century. The interior (an area of 153 x 38 x 90 m) is divided into a nave and two aisles of grouped piers. The style is Gothic with ogival arches and cross vaults, and bare architectural lines highlighted by the white plaster and the spare ornamentation.

The artists who contributed to the decoration were Lorenzo Ghiberti, Paolo Uccello, Tino di Camaino, Nanni di Banco, and Benedetto da Maiano. Two frescoes are famous: one done for Niccolò da Tolentino by Andrea del Castagno (1456), and the other for Giovanni Acuto by Paolo Uccello (1436). The dome was frescoed by Vasari with the "Last Judgement"; the choir (1555) was designed by Baccio Bandinelli; the bas-reliefs that adorn the urn of San Zanobi are by Lorenzo Ghiberti.

The New Sacristy is the place where, on 26 April 1478, Lorenzo de' Medici, known as the Magnificent, protected by his followers, succeeded in escaping during the Pazzi Conspiracy while his brother Giuliano was killed. The **bell tower** by Giotto is 81.75 m. tall and was built by three architects, Giotto, Andrea Pisano and Francesco Talenti who succeeded each other between 1334 and 1359. The construction is original for the simplicity of its style. Rich marbles underscore the geometrical form, on which the Gothic style is grafted for decorative effects.

Cathedral Museum.
Luca della Robbia, the Singing Gallery (det.).

CATHEDRAL MUSEUM

The Cathedral Museum located at n° 9, Piazza Duomo, is where works taken from the Baptistery, Cathedral and Bell Tower to protect them against the elements are displayed. The statue of Pope Boniface VIII and the group of the Madonna and Child are thirteenth-century works by Arnolfo di Cambio. The statue of Saint John is by Donatello, the sculptor who, in the 15th century, revealed the human body drawing inspiration from the classical world of Greece and Rome. He transformed Gothic statuary by emphasising the expression of feelings.

The Pietà, with Nicodemus upholding the body of Christ just taken down from the Cross, the Virgin Mary and Mary Magdalene, was done by Michelangelo in 1550 for his tomb. The sculptor portrayed himself as Nicodemus, holding Christ's body. His face hidden in the dark shadow of his hood: he is an old man, with a weary stance, no longer capable of carrying the heavy body. The Virgin mother chosen by the Holy Spirit, is racked with grief, and with Mary

Statue of Saint John.

Magdalene, who is portrayed in all her materiality, she helps him accept human destiny serenely. The choir galleries by Donatello and Luca della Robbia are considered masterpieces, as are Donatello's statues of Jeremiah, called the Popolano, and of Habbakuk called the Zuccone; both of these works are vivified by powerful spirituality. On the walls of the adjoining room are 36 panels that were once on the bell tower. They show *The Creation of Adam and Eve*, *Working of the Land* and *The Arts* portrayed with human figures transformed into symbols or with realistic scenes.

These include Harvesting, Ploughing and Navigation, which have an immediate appeal because of the perfect blend of form and content. The sculptors who executed these works over a period that spanned two hundred years, included Andrea Pisano, Andrea Orcagna and Luca della Robbia. The panels carved by Ghiberti and his assistants for the Gate of Paradise, from the Baptistery, can be seen in the other room.

Lorenzo Ghiberti (1378-1455)

Ghiberti achieved fame as a sculptor and goldsmith when he won the competition held for the decoration and casting of the North Door of the Baptistery. The work was acclaimed as showing great artistic value, and as a result he was entrusted to decorate the second door - the East Door - without holding a competition. The bas-reliefs on it were of such superior quality that Michelangelo defined the door as "worthy of Paradise".

Gate of Paradise. Lorenzo Ghiberti, self-portrait.

The **Baptistery** of Saint John dates back to the 11th century and was preceded by various buildings in the same area. In 1330, Andrea Pisano completed the decoration of the South Door with panels portraying scenes of the life of St. John the Baptist. Lorenzo Ghiberti was commissioned to do the North Door from 1403-1424 and the East Door from 1425-1452. The reliefs of the East Door are an expression of the passage from the Gothic to the Humanist spirit. The scenes are sculptured, the compositions appear detached from the preceding schemes, the figures move freely, the landscapes are illuminated with a new light, air blows through the trees and leaves and over the fields. All of Florence flocked in front of this door, defined by Michelangelo as "worthy of Paradise", to show their enthusiasm. Among the important figures present were: Cosimo the Elder, Lorenzo Valla, Marsilio Ficino, Leonardo Bruni, Lorenzo the Magnificent, Botticelli, Poliziano, and Girolamo Savonarola. Inside, the Baptistery opens into a breathtaking space, in both its size and its decoration and mosaics covering the upper walls. The marble and flooring are extraordinary. The thirteenth-century mosaics portray the Last Judgement.

Piazza del Duomo.

DAVID

ACADEMY GALLERY

UFFIZI GALLERY

ALLEGORY OF SPRING

BY MICHELANGELO

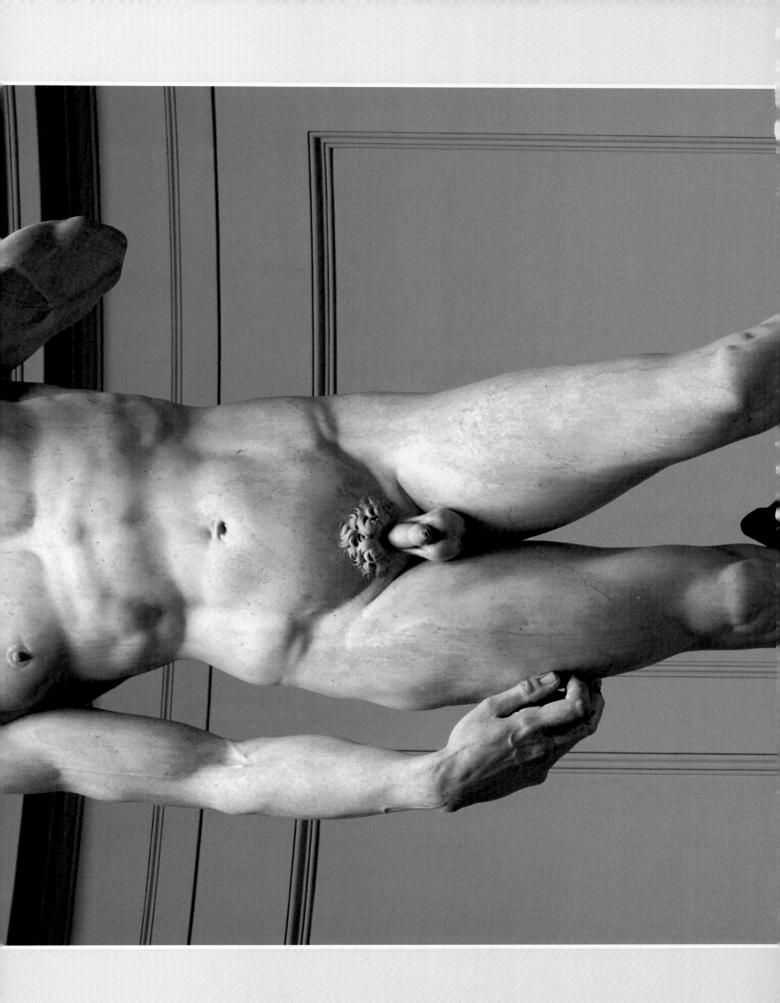

BY *SANDRO BOTTICELLI*

Creation of Adam and Eve.

The work of man.
The Sacrifice of Cain and Abel.

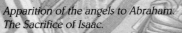

Noah's Drunkenness.

Apparition of the angels to Abraham.
The Sacrifice of Isaac.

Esau and Jacob.

Joseph sold by his Brethren.
the cup is discovered in Benjamin's sack.
The Taking of Jericho.

Moses receives the Law.

War against the Philistines, the Death of Goliath.

Solomon and the Queen of Sheba.

Cosimo the Elder (1389-1464)

He was an absolute ruler in a city extremely jealous of its freedom. Generous in the promotion of the letters and arts, he was the patron of Donatello, Brunelleschi, Ghiberti, Luca della Robbia and others. On his death, the Florentines honoured him with the title of "Pater Patriae", engraved on his tomb in the Church of San Lorenzo.

Uffizi Gallery. Botticelli, Adoration of the Magi.
Portrait of Cosimo the Elder.

Palazzo Medici-Riccardi, chapel.
Benozzo Gozzoli, Journey of the Magi to Bethlehem

Monastery of St. Mark.
Fra Angelico Museum, The Flight into Egypt.

Monastery of St. Mark. Fra Angelico Museum
the washing of the feet.

CONVENT OF ST. MARK

Piazza della Santissima Annunziata is the square between the portico of the Foundling Hospital, the portico of the Santissima Annunziata and the portico of the Brotherhood of the Servants of Mary. An equestrian statue of Ferdinand I (1587-1609) stands in the centre.

Brunelleschi built the **Foundling Hospital** between 1419-1434. Slender columns and airy arches stand out on the high steps, supporting the trabeation, and the wall above is characterised by elegant windows. In 1463, Andrea della Robbia set ten round glazed ceramic tiles in white on a blue background in the pendentives, with putti - the children who found refuge inside - as subjects.

The **Santissima Annunziata** preserves only three sections of the building designed by Michelozzo: the atrium, a small chapel and the Cloister of the Dead. Decoration consists of the *Nativity* by Andrea del Sarto, the monument to Orlando de' Medici by Bernardo Rossellino (1456), the Pietà by Baccio Bandinelli, and two frescoes by Andrea del Castagno. Cellini, Pontormo, Franciabigio, Andrea del Sarto and Giambologna are buried in this church.

The Church and Convent of San Marco, where Giovanni Pico della Mirandola (1463-1494) and Angelo Ambrosini, known as Poliziano, are buried, are located in **Piazza San Marco.**

The Medici ordered the construction of the church, cloisters and library of San Marco, and later the Church of San Lorenzo, as a burial place for the family. The Palazzo where they lived was along the road joining the two. The road, formerly known as Via Larga, is now Via Cavour.

The **Convent of San Marco** maintains a tangible feeling of serenity in its cells, cloisters, in the frescoes of Fra Angelico and the library. The walls can be seen from the piazza and they open into a series of tall narrow windows; one enters the porticoed cloister, with large meeting rooms along the sides and, on the first floor, the small cells of the friars and the library designed and executed by Michelozzo between 1437-1452. The library is a long room, with double arches on columns. The glass cabinets contain richly illuminated and rare antiphonaries and psalters. Faith and mysticism emanate from the frescoes by Fra Angelico, who painted in the convent between 1435-1445. The most significant works are the two *Annunciations*, the one on the wall above the stairs and the other in the third cell in the left corridor. In the Fra Angelico Museum, on the ground floor, the *Descent from the Cross* and the *Last Judgement* are arresting works, as is the *Crucifixion* in the Chapter Hall. The *Last Supper* by Domenico Ghirlandaio can be seen on the ground floor.

Michelangelo Buonarroti *(1475-1564)*

A pupil of Domenico Ghirlandaio, following the master's recommendation he was accepted as an apprentice in the Medici Garden. On Lorenzo de' Medici's death he fled to Bologna, and from here he reached Rome. His works such as St. Peter's dome, the frescoes of the "Creation" and the "Last Judgement" in the Sistine Chapel, and the statues of David and Moses are masterpieces of universal interest.

Florence, Academy Gallery. Daniele da Volterra, bust of Michelangelo.

ACADEMY GALLERY

Academy Gallery. the Adimari chest.

Academy Gallery.
Michelangelo, Pietà of Palestrina.

The Academy Gallery is renowned for the David by Michelangelo, the marble statue visible at the end of the entrance. Michelangelo sculpted the statue during his first period of activity from 1501 to 1504, immediately showing his abandonment of classical imitation and anatomy. In his later works he began to express the idea that the beauty of the body is a manifestation of God and the soul. From a technical point of view, the task of the sculptor was to liberate the figure from the mass of marble by removing the waste that was enclosing it. The statues of the *Prisoners* (1518), sculpted for the tomb of Julius II, and the *Pietà of Palestrina* of the same period are displayed in the corridor. The sense of tragedy that derives from looking at this group is given by the two Marys in the act of holding the body of Christ, which is falling. The paintings displayed in the adjoining rooms are by painters of the 13th and 14th centuries. The *Adimari chest* is famous for the portrayal of a wedding feast of the time. The *Annunciation* by Lorenzo Monaco, the *Madonna of the Sea* by Sandro Botticelli, the *Apparition of the Virgin to St. Bernard* by Fra Bartolomeo, and the *Madonna del Pozzo* by Franciabigio, are works from the 15th-16th century.

New Sacristy. Michelangelo, Night
Michelangelo, Dawn.

PALAZZO MEDICI-RICCARDI

The Palazzo **Medici-Riccardi** was the residence of the Medici from the time of Cosimo the Elder, who commissioned the building to Michelozzo, to the Grand Dukes. The building is characterised by ashlar-work, which becomes more dressed from the ground floor towards the top, by the stone bench in sandstone and the cornice. The Medici Museum, reached from the courtyard, is in the rooms where Lorenzo the Magnificent had his bedroom and study, near the external corner loggia that no longer exists. There are several portraits, works of art and various mementos including the funeral mask of Lorenzo the Magnificent, in the museum.

The **chapel** of the palazzo, located on the first floor and transformed in the 17th century contains the fresco of the *Journey of the Magi to Bethlehem* by Benozzo Gozzoli (1459-1460). Personalities belonging to the Medici family and other nobles who took part in the ride to meet the scholars coming from Ferrara can be noted.

The **Church of San Lorenzo** is an imposing building (Brunelleschi, Donatello; 1420-1460), and it has no façade. The interior emanates a pleasing feeling of tranquillity and contains several works of art of inestimable value, such as the *Tabernacle* by Desiderio da Settignano (1428-1464) and the pulpits by Donatello. The Old Sacristy is the result of a collaboration between Brunelleschi, Donatello and other artists. Donatello worked on the medallions, tondi and doors (1435-1443). In 1472, Verrocchio did the tomb of Giovanni and Pietro, sons of Cosimo the Elder, whose parents are buried in the centre of the room.

New Sacristy. Michelangelo, Day.

Michelangelo, Twilight.

SAN LORENZO. THE NEW SACRISTY

Michelangelo worked at the New Sacristy from 1523 al 1531, and with the statues of the Day and Night, of Dawn and Twilight, he expressed the concept of "fugit tempus". Set on the slanted cover and curled up along the edges of the sepulchres, the statues express resignation to the passing of time without expectations and without hope. And these statues are the images of persons who dominated in life. The tombs of Giuliano and Lorenzo the Magnificent are against the wall at the entry, on the left is the sepulchre of Lorenzo II, Duke of Urbino, grandson of Lorenzo the Magnificent, with the statues of Dawn and Twilight. Opposite is the sepulchre of Giuliano, son of Lorenzo the Magnificent, with the statues of Day and Night.

The statues express the concept in an evident way: the Thought in which Lorenzo is absorbed begins with Dawn and terminates with Twilight, the Action of the Day terminates with Night. Thought and Action occur within a period of one day, and then slip into the sepulchre. The **Chapel of the Princes** also expresses a moment of the spirit: the chapel, on an octagonal plan dominated by an octagonal dome, was executed as a sepulchral monument for the Grand Dukes, whose coffins lie below in the crypt. It is a rich and splendid room. The **Laurentian Library** was built between 1524-1578 by order of Pope Clement VII on a plan by Michelangelo; it is composed of a vestibule, stairway and hall. The nobility of the architectural style recalls the importance of the collection of manuscripts and documents that the Medici had gathered from the time of Cosimo the Elder, including the acts of the Council for the Reunification of the Churches.

BARGELLO NATIONAL MUSEUM

*Bargello National Museum.
Giambologna, Mercury.*

*Bargello National Museum.
Donatello, Saint George.*

*Bargello National Museum.
Donatello, David.*

The Bargello was built in the mid-thirteenth century and still maintains its typical fourteenth-century appearance given by the projections, Gothic windows, and Guelph battlements on small arches. The collection of sculptures displayed in its rooms forms the National Bargello Museum famous for masterpieces of sculpture from the fifteenth and sixteenth centuries.

In the hall next to the entrance one can see several works by Michelangelo, among which the *Brutus* (1540) stands out, characterised by the head tilted in a defiant attitude. The tondo of the Virgin and Child is distinctive for the different levels on which the figures are sculpted. The courtyard maintains an unmistakable fourteenth-century imprint with coats of arms and frescoes on the walls, and the open stairway, executed between 1345-1367 by Neri di Fioravanti. The bronze statue of Mercury, a masterpiece by Giambologna, is displayed in the loggia. For its size, architectural divisions and large window, the council hall betrays its fourteenth-century style. Several sculptures are displayed here, gathered from various parts of the city. From the first half of the 15th century: St. George, the Young St. John from the Martelli house, David, St. John the Baptist, the Marzocco, Attis, the bust of Niccolò da Uzzano by Donatello. The bronze David, portrays the figure of a young man, with a richly carved body, in a resting position after having cut off the head of Goliath: it is the first nude since Roman and Greek times, done by Donatello for Cosimo the Elder in 1430. On the second floor equally famous works can be admired: Verrocchio's David; Hercules and Antaeus with nimble lines, by Antonio del Pollaiuolo; the bust of Matteo Palmieri by Antonio Rossellino; the bust of Pietro Mellini by Benedetto da Maiano. The Ressman arms collection completes the exhibit.

Church of Santa Maria Novella, Main Chapel.
Domenico Ghirlandaio,
Apparition of the angel to Saint Zachary in the temple.

Church of Santa Maria Novella. Interior.

CHURCH OF SANTA MARIA NOVELLA

Set in the façade and along the side of the Basilica of Santa Maria Novella are Gothic-Romanesque sepulchres from the 14th century. The doorway, the crowning, and the connecting volutes are in the Renaissance style (Leon Battista Alberti, 15th century). The church is rich in tradition and works of art. In the 15th century, the Council Fathers held meetings there for the Reunification of the Churches. The frescoes in the Filippo Strozzi Chapel are by Filippino Lippi; in the Main Chapel the frescoes are by Domenico Ghirlandaio and his assistants including Michelangelo (1485-1490). Then there are the Gondi Chapel and the Strozzi Chapel with frescoes by Nardo di Cione (14th century) and the Trinity by Masaccio. The Green Cloister built in 1350, so-called because of its predominantly green frescoes by Paolo Uccello with scenes from the Old Testament. One then enters the Great Spanish Chapel (1359) with its frescoed walls by Andrea di Bonaiuto.

BASILICA OF SANTA CROCE

The Basilica of Santa Croce is a Gothic church dating from the 13th century with a nave and two side aisles, an Egyptian-cross layout with transept, octagonal pillars, and lancet arches. The interior is immense, rich with works of art and funeral monuments, including the tombs of Michelangelo (16th century) and Niccolò Machiavelli, the tomb of Leonardo Bruni by Bernardo Rossellino, and the monument to Carlo Marsuppini, by Desiderio da Settignano. Donatello, the *Annunciation*; the Peruzzi Chapel, with frescoes by Giotto depicting scenes from the life of St. John the Baptist and St. John the Evangelist. In the cloister, the fourteenth-century side of the church and the façade of the Pazzi Chapel on which Brunelleschi worked from 1430 to 1445, leaving it unfinished, are remarkable. The Cathedral Museum is located in the old refectory, where the remains of frescoes, sculptures and paintings once in the cathedral are preserved, including Cimabue's famous *Crucifixion* restored after the flood.

Basilica of Santa Croce, monument to Michelangelo.

Basilica of Santa Croce, Choir Chapel.

Basilica of Santa Croce, interior.

Church of Santa Maria del Carmine, Brancacci Chapel.
Masaccio, The Expulsion of Adam and Eve.

Church of Santa Maria del Carmine, Brancacci Chapel.
Masolino da Panicale, The Expulsion of Adam and Eve.

Masaccio *(1401-1428)*

He is considered the first painter to adhere to the new Renaissance style, as can be seen in the Church of Santa Maria del Carmine. Masaccio worked here in the Brancacci Chapel together with his teacher, Masolino da Panicale, and the works here allow the two masters to be compared. Masaccio's power of expression is emphasised in the scenes of the expulsion from the Garden of Eden and in the Payment of the Tribute.

Brancacci Chapel. Masaccio, self-portrait.

CHURCH OF SANTA MARIA DEL CARMINE

The Convent of Santa Maria del Carmine was part of a large group of sacred sites. The church, of medieval origin, was rebuilt in 1771 after a fire that spared only the Brancacci Chapel, of which the frescoed wall decorations constitute one of the valuable testimonies of Italian painting. The decoration of the chapel was begun by the late-Gothic painter Masolino da Panicale, on commission of the merchant Felice Brancacci; continued by Masaccio around 1425 and completed between 1474 and 1485 by Filippino Lippi. The scenes narrate episodes of the life of St. Peter with details of the Original Sin. The scene of the Tribute takes place in three episodes against the background of the Pratomagno where the figures of the Apostles are gathered in a circle around Christ. The figures appear to blend with the panorama and the same colours are used for both. Christ tells Peter that he will find money in the fish's mouth, and the action begins and concludes with a succession of fatal movements virtually without respite. Peter finds the coin and pays the tax collector.

Masaccio was one of the greatest artists of Florentine painting. He died mysteriously in Rome very young. Nevertheless, he successfully followed Giotto's teachings and surpassed them. The dynamism and perspective of the figures in his paintings unite style and concept to express the wholeness of mankind associated with the fascinating moment of the Creation.

Galileo Galilei *(1564-1642)*

He was studying medicine at the University of Pisa when, in 1581, observing a lamp as it swayed back and forth he noticed that it took the same amount of time: he had discovered the isochronism of the pendulum. He wrote, among other works, the "Dialogue concerning the Two Chief World Systems", which brought him both fame and grief. He was excommunicated and isolated because his theories contrasted with Church doctrine. He adopted the method of experimentation based on calculation and the careful observation of results obtained.

Pitti Gallery. Justus Sustermans, Portrait of Galileo.

Pisa, Campo dei Miracoli.

Giovanni Pisano, pulpit. Figures of virtues.

Pisa, Leaning Tower.

PISA

The Campo dei Miracoli is undoubtedly an architectural complex unique in the world, planned and commissioned by the Pisans to celebrate the victory of the fleet against the Muslims in Palermo in 1063. A uniform style characterises the entire group; the first building to be planned by Buschetto di Giovanni, who was in charge of work from 1063 until the end of the century, was the Cathedral dedicated to the Virgin. A Crucifix by Giambologna stands on the high altar, enriched with polychrome marble. The mosaics of the apse portray Christ with the Virgin and the Baptist, the work of Cimabue and Lapo. The Gothic-style pulpit is by Giovanni Pisano. In 1153, Diotisalvi began work for the construction of the **Baptistery**, done in the Romanesque

style with decorations and Gothic elements from a later period. The building in white marble is circular and exterior decoration covers the three storeys. The dome is pyramidal. In the interior, four large pillars and eight columns placed in between support the large arches, sustaining the women's gallery. Guido Bigarelli da Como did the octagonal Baptismal Font in 1246. The most remarkable work of the Baptistery, however, is the pulpit by Nicola Pisano, of 1260. The **Leaning Tower**, or the Tower of Pisa, is famous throughout the world for its slant. It was built between 1173 and the end of the fourteenth century. The circular plan is entirely covered with white marble with six orders of arcades. The **Cemetery** is the most recent part of the complex, and the white marble gallery that surrounds it took nearly two centuries of work, from 1277 to 1464, to complete.

SIENA

Piazza del Campo is one of the most unusual mediaeval piazzas in Italy. The city centre and the stage for the well-known Palio, it is the true heart of the city. Piazza del Campo has an extraordinary semicircular concave shape, the design of which recalls the shape of a shell. The optical effect is quite astonishing due to the uneven ground, transformed here into a masterpiece, in which every building was constructed for a precise aesthetic reason, in order to achieve a controlled circular form. Laid with special bricks arranged to form a fishbone pattern, the piazza dates back to 1347. It is a superb "reception area" and its division recalls the period of the Republic. The segments are divided by lines of white stone to recall the famous government of nine. The first building to be erected in the piazza was the Palazzo

Siena, Cathedral, inlaid flooring. Pinturicchio, Crates.
Siena. Palazzo Pubblico and Mangia Tower.

Pubblico, built at the end of the 13th century. The Map Room contains "Maestà" the fresco by Simone Martini, completed in 1315. The other fresco in the room, "*Guidoriccio da Fogliano at the siege of Montemassi*" (1328), is also by the same artist. Construction of the Mangia Tower was begun by the brothers Minuccio and Francesco Naldi in 1338 and completed only ten years later. The Fonte Gaia, sculpted by Jacopo della Quercia between 1409 and 1419, is situated in Piazza del Campo opposite the Palazzo Pubblico. The imposing building of Nicola Pisano from the second half of the thirteenth-century overlooks Piazza del Duomo. Built on the top of the hill on which the historical town centre of Siena expanded, it dominates the entire city with its majestic dome. The façade was executed by Giovanni Pisano. The interior is grandiose and well lit; the plan in a Latin

Palio. The Mossa Curve.

Cathedral, Piccolomini Library. Three Graces.

cross is divided into a nave and two aisles with breath-taking massive marble columns with horizontal fascia in black and white. The bell tower of the Cathedral was built in Romanesque style in 1313 on a plan by Agostino and Agnolo di Ventura. The Cathedral Museum contains works of art coming from the Cathedral and from other churches of the dioceses of Siena, including the "Maestà" of Duccio di Boninsegna and paintings by Pietro Lorenzetti.

The Palio of Siena is the most important event of the city and is a perfect visiting card for Italy worldwide. Both a religious and a civil festival, it is not just an historical commemoration, but is much more: it is the essence of the city of Siena. The winning contrada is given the "cencio", a standard bearing the effigy of the Madonna.

Rome

In Rome, capital of the Roman Empire and of Christianity, one can see the most important artistic creations of the religious world. The Roman Empire extended its dominion from the Persian Gulf to Britannia passing through Asia, Africa and Europe. In 721 B.C., the year of the mythical foundation of Rome, the shepherds descended from their huts on the Palatine Hill where they lived and set out to conquer the peoples of the world, barbarians and civilised alike. As legionaries they constructed ports, roads, bridges, tunnels, aqueducts and theatres and built thousands of kilo-

Rome from the Pincio Park with Piazza del Popolo and the Dome of St. Peter

metres of walls. Many European, African and Middle Eastern cities were constructed with the plan of the castra, or camps of the Roman Legions. During the centuries of the invasions, the destroyed and plundered monuments were covered under heaps of rubble that resurfaced at the beginning of the Middle Ages. Works of art of all kinds then appeared: statues and paintings that form the core of museums worldwide or can be admired relocated in churches, palazzi and monuments. Rome, built by a race of conquerors, had the vibrant centre of Roman life in the Forum, a name that derives from *outside* the Palatine walls. Roman Emperors transformed Rome into the largest and most highly developed city in the ancient world. Towards the end of the 14th century the needs of Catholicism called for radical transformations to the city and St. Peter's became the new centre. The political, commercial and religious changes of the 16th century attracted many artists to Rome around the Vatican, where the artistic tradition of Florence was carried on by Michelangelo, Raphael, and Leonardo da Vinci, who moved to Rome.

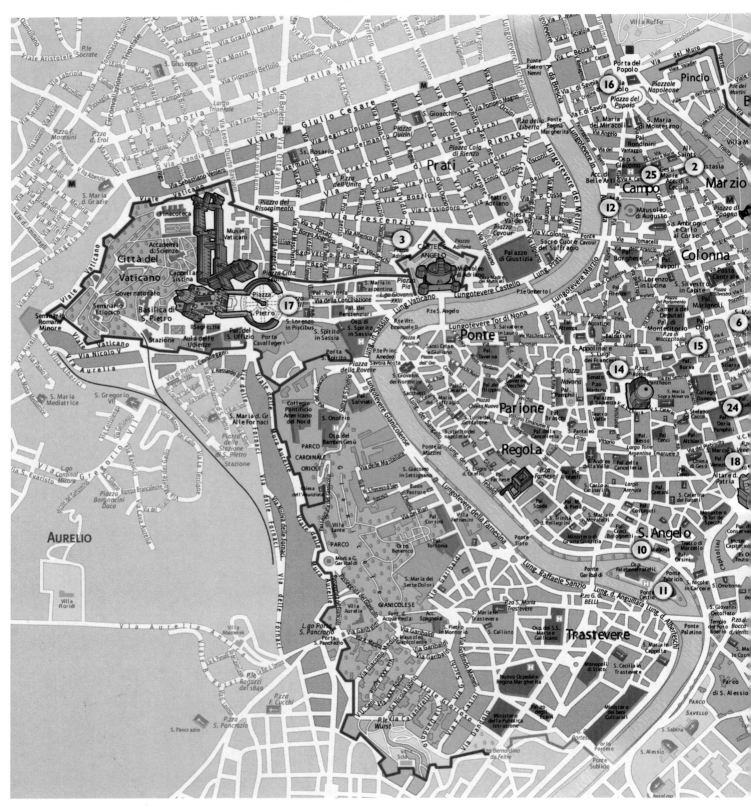

1) Arch of Constantine
2) Campus Martius
3) Castel Sant' Angelo
4) Colosseum

5) Domus Aurea
6) Trevi Fountain
7) Imperial Forums
8) Roman Forum

9) Borghese Gallery
10) Ghetto
11) Island in the Tiber
12) Mausoleum of Augustus

13) Palatine
14) Pantheon
15) Piazza Colonna
16) Piazza del Popolo

EMPERORS

Gaius Julius Caesar (102-44 B.C.). One of the great conquerors of ancient times he anticipated the transition from the Republic to the Empire and lost his life attempting to achieve this.

Gaius Julius Caesar Octavian Augustus (63 B.C.-14). He completed the work of Caesar. He decreed the new religion of the Emperor-God transforming himself into the symbol of the Empire and God's mediator

Nero Claudius Caesar Germanicus (37-68). Nero was the emperor who was attributed with bloody deeds with the sole objective of satisfying material pleasures.

Titus Flavius Vespasian (9-79). With his sons Titus and Domitian, he conquered the Judea and razed the temple of Jerusalem to the ground. He had the Jewish prisoners build the Colosseum in Rome.

Marcus Ulpius Trajan (53-117). An excellent legion commander, with the construction of the Trajan Forum and numerous civil works, he contributed to the transformation of the city plan of Rome.

Publius Aelius Hadrianus (76-138). A highly cultured emperor with a sharp mind, he visited the territories of the Empire and spent long periods in Greece and Egypt. The monuments he planned often reflect obscure concepts.

Marcus Aurelius Antoninus (121-180). A follower of Stoic philosophy, he enacted laws in support of the State becoming a ruthless persecutor of Christians who did not accept the religion of the Emperor-God.

Gaius Aurelius Valerius Diocletian (245-313). The vastness of the Empire and increasing difficulties in keeping the barbarians outside the borders, forced him to share power among two Augusti and two Caesars

Constantine (280-337). He promoted Christianity ensuring its pre-eminent position by giving a considerable fortune in thanks for the support he had received during the battles that gained him the Empire. He transferred the capital to Byzantium.

17) St. Peter's Square

18) Piazza Venezia

19) Ludovisi Quarter

20) Gardens of Sallust

21) Quirinal

22) Santa Maria Maggiore

23) Baths of Diocletian

24) Baths of Caracalla

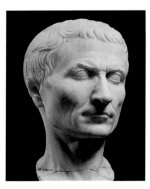

Gaius Julius Caesar *(102-44 B.C.)*

General, pontifex, statesman, and writer. He married Cornelia, conquered Gaul (58-51 B.C.), and won the Civil War (49-45 B.C.). He lived with Cleopatra, who gave him a son (47 B.C.). He destroyed Pompey and his legions. He drew up building plans for Rome, as well as plans to drain the Pontine Marshes, Lake Fucino and reconstruct Carthage. He was stabbed to death in 44 B.C.

Pisa, Cathedral Museum. Julius Caesar.

Location of the monuments.
1) Curia. 2) Temple of Saturn. 3) Basilica Julia
4) Temple of the Dioscuri. 5) Temple of Divus Julius.

ROMAN FORUM

The **Curia** was the seat of the Senate from Tullius Hostilius, 680 B.C., to the 5th century A.D. and it was converted into a church in 625. The interior contained the statue of Victory, the seats of the senators and curule tribunes and, at the entrance, the bronze doorway. The Comitium, where the populace gathered for the sessions of the Senate, was in front of the façade. The **Temple of Castor and Pollux** (484 B.C.), was dedicated to the Dioscuri, the brothers who had fought alongside the Romans in the Battle of Lake Regillus. It was a temple in a harmonious style embellished with Corinthian columns. The **Temple of Saturn** (497 B.C.) was an imposing building, as the remaining columns and architrave show. The State Treasury was kept inside, plundered many times over the centuries, lastly by Julius Caesar on his return from the campaign in Gaul, in order to pay the legionaries left without wages. The Saturnalian Feast began with an impressive ceremony in this temple. This raucous event was one of the most exhilarating of Roman traditions. The Saturnalia, dedicated to Saturn, the god of fertility, took place from 17 to 23 December, a time of rest and awakening of nature. During this period the entire population of Rome enjoyed the right of equality: slaves took advantage of the occasion to reproach their masters' vices and faults, and they participated together in the banquets.

Roman Forum. Curia.

Roman Forum. Curia, interior.

Roman Forum. Temple of Saturn.

Shakespeare, Julius Caesar, Act 3, Scene 2. Funeral oration of Antony in the Roman Forum in honour of Caesar.

Friends, Romans, countrymen, lend me your ears; / I come to bury Caesar, not to praise him. / The evil that men do lives after them; / The good is oft interred with their bones; /So let it be with Caesar. The noble Brutus / Hath told you Caesar was ambitious. / If it were so, it was a grievous fault; / And grievously hath Caesar answer'd it. /Here, under leave of Brutus and the rest- / For Brutus is an honourable man; / So are they all, all honourable men- / Come I to speak in Caesar's funeral. / He was my friend, faithful and just to me; / But Brutus says he was ambitious, / And Brutus is an honourable man. / He hath brought many captives home to Rome, / Whose ransoms did the general coffers fill; / Did this in Caesar seem ambitious? /

When that the poor have cried, Caesar hath wept; / Ambition should be made of sterner stuff. / Yet Brutus says he was ambitious; / And Brutus is an honourable man. / You all did see that on the Lupercal / I thrice presented him a kingly crown, / Which he did thrice refuse. Was this ambition? / Yet Brutus says he was ambitious; / And sure he is an honourable man. / I speak not to disprove what Brutus spoke, / But here I am to speak what I do know. / You all did love him once, not without cause; / What cause withholds you, then, to mourn for him? / O judgment! thou art fled to brutish beasts, / And men have lost their reason! Bear with me; / My heart is in the coffin there with Caesar, / And I must pause till it come back to me.

Octavian, Augustus Gaius Julius Caesar *(63 B.C.-14).*

He formed the second triumvirate with Antony and Lepidus. In the naval battle of Actium he defeated Antony and Cleopatra. He obtained the position of Pontifex Maximus and the title of Pater Patriae, bringing peace to the territories of the Empire. He decreed the State religion in honour of Rome and the Emperor, symbol of the Empire, was deified. With the help of Agrippa, Maecenas and Livia he transformed Rome from a city of brick into city of marble. He had a temple to Caesar built in the Forum.

Capitoline Museum, Emperors' Room. Octavian.

Location of the monuments.
1) Mausoleum of Augustus 2) Ara Pacis. 3) Forum of Augustus.

Ara Pacis Augustae. A procession of members of the Royal House.

Ara Pacis Augustae. Symbols of prosperity.

Augustus was informed of Caesar's murder in the Middle East and together with Agrippa, his esteemed counsellor and friend, he returned to Rome.

He forced Antony to hand over the testament and the legacy passed on by Caesar, and he urged Cleopatra to leave Rome with Caesarion, the son she had by Caesar. He then gave orders to kill the 400 senators who had participated in the conspiracy against Caesar, pursued the others who had barricaded themselves in Perugia, and razed the city to the ground.

The **Forum of Augustus** was built to commemorate the Battle of Philippi where Cassius and Brutus, Caesar's assassins, were defeated. Of this Forum there remains the stairway that leads to the temple, two basilicas, and a few columns. Eight columns enriched the temple, called the Temple of Mars Ultor or vindicator. The Emperor had statues of the Romans who had honoured the country placed in the apses of the arcades.

Ara Pacis Augustae. The Senate had voted in favour of the monument in 13 B.C., following the campaigns in Spain and Gaul, to celebrate the glory of the Emperor. It is

Forum of Augustus.

made up of an altar and marble slabs carved with fine artwork. Over the centuries several slabs were broken, others were lost and discovered buried under the buildings that stood in Campus Martius. Some of them were gathered and preserved in suitable places, while others were again removed and transferred to the Louvre in Paris and to Villa Medici in Rome, belonging to France. The reliefs illustrate the course of the procession in which personalities of the Imperial Family with Augustus, Livia, Agrippa and Maecenas took part. The exploits of Augustus are described in the nearby monument of Ancyranum.

Mausoleum of Augustus. The construction built in Campus Martius, outside the city walls, had a circular form, with a foundation of 89 meters and a height of 44. Its interior contained documents, plans, statues, paintings and the ashes of Augustus, Livia, Octavia, Marcellus, Agrippa and the other personalities of the Julius Claudius family, who had held the fate of the Roman Empire in their hands. The radical destruction is one of the most serious losses for the knowledge of periods among the most glorious of human civilisation; all that is left is a circular foundation furrowed with corridors that lead to the cell.

Nero Claudius Caesar Germanicus (37-68)

The psychologically disturbed nature of Nero's political activity is one of a weak man; he lived fighting against the senators using the accusation of lese majesty to get rid of them and confiscate their property. His mother, Agrippina, a woman who craved power decided for him, and under her influence Nero betrayed his friends, squandered public funds, and accused the Christians of setting fire to Rome. He committed suicide at the age of 31, unable to confront the trial the senators had brought against him.

Capitoline Museum, Emperors' Room. Nero.

Location of the monuments.
1) Domus Aurea. 2) Colosseum. 3) Arch of Constantine.

The **Great Fire of Rome.** The Great Fire of Rome broke out the night of 18 July 64 A.D., in the south-east corner of the Circus Maximus. The fire spread quickly due to the strong wind and the wooden structure of the houses, blazing for an entire week. In the end three districts of the city were destroyed and another seven were badly damaged. From the information that has reached us, there is not the slightest proof of Nero's guilt. Indeed, it seems that the Emperor provided help to the families affected by the fire. The Christians were held responsible and many of them lost their lives, including Peter and Paul. Their bodies, covered with pitch and impaled, were used to illuminate the paths of the Domus Aurea. Once the fire was extinguished, Nero designed a detailed plan for reconstruction based on the widening of the roads, setting a limit in height for new buildings and setting aside vast areas as gardens. The reconstruction was considered Rome's first city plan.

The people who for various reasons were connected with Nero were his mother Agrippina, Octavia, his first wife whom he married when she was 16, Poppaea, wife of Otho, Statilia, Messalina, Seneca, Burrus, and Tigellinus. These names enrich his bibliography already on the dark side. Nero, however, was lovingly protected by Acte, the woman who deposited his ashes in the Domitians' family tomb, located on the slopes of the Pincian hill, in the area where the Church of Santa Maria del Popolo now stands.

Palatine. Imperial palaces

Domus Aurea. Octagonal Room, ambulatory

Domus Aurea. To construct the buildings that were intended to glorify the greatness of the Empire and the magnanimity of the Emperor, Nero chose a vast area between the Esquiline and the Palatine, and commissioned the architects Severus and Celerus to design and carry out the work. The number of buildings and gardens, roads and services needed to achieve the city plan meant years of work and provoked discontent among the population. The main building had a large façade facing the lake and forums: in front of the entrance stood a huge statue of Nero, called the Colossus, which gave its name to the following construction, the Colosseum. The interior was enriched with magnificent rooms like the Golden Vault for which the most advanced technical discoveries were applied to the windows and the various decorations. When guests sat down at the table, for example, a light drizzle of perfumes descended over their heads. After 1,500 years some painters entered these grottoes to copy and reproduce the decorations which came to be known as grotesques, from the word "grotto".

"The time has now come for you to find a home in Veio, because there is no longer any room here".

This is how the people voiced their disapproval of the endless protraction of the construction of Nero's Domus Aurea.

Titus Flavius Vespasian *(9-79).*

As the first Emperor of the Gens Flavia, he demonstrated excellent abilities as a legion commander on the Rhine, in Africa and in Judea. Supported by the legionaries, he was elected Emperor. His son, Titus, named as his father's successor, conquered and destroyed Jerusalem. Vespasian sent Agricola to resume the conquest of Britannia. The Colosseum was built during his rule.

Capitoline Museum, Emperors' Room. Vespasian.

Colosseum.   Gladiators.

The **Colosseum.** The construction of the amphitheatre was begun by Vespasian in 72, continued under Titus and completed in its upper part by Domitian in 82. The Colosseum is elliptical in shape (188 x 156 x 57 m high); the arena is 76 x 46 m. The tiers of seats had a capacity of about 50,000 spectators. An impos-

Roman Forum. Arch of Titus.

Roman Forum, Arch of Titus. Triumph (detail).

ing structure, it rose on three orders of arcades in the Doric, Ionic and Corinthian style surmounted by an attic with fretworked ashlars on the outside of it, holding the brackets of the velarium covering. The tiers of steps of the cavea were built between the arena and the external wall; benches were provided for women above. A place in the cavea was reserved for members of the equestrian order, citizens, and the common people. Each spectator was issued a pass with a seat number. The entries reserved for the passage of the authorities were under the archways of the ellipse, those for the entry of the gladiators - called "Sanavivaria" - near the Foro della Pace, and one called "Libitinaria" for the carts that carried off the bodies of the gladiators and wild beasts. The basement served as a storeroom and menagerie. The Colosseum was used for games that, during its inauguration, lasted 100 days, during which 50,000 wild animals were killed. It was used up to the fifteenth century.

Arch of Titus. Domitian had the arch built in 81, in honour of his father Vespasian and brother Titus, to commemorate their victories against the Jews and the destruction of the Temple of Jerusalem. It has a single fornix and is embellished with finely made sculptures. Among them one of the most well-known depicts the Triumph of Titus, in which the Jews taken prisoner drag the cart on which the menorah stands out. It later became the symbol of the Jewish nation.

The **gladiator** was a prisoner of war forced into slavery, and as such, sold at a price calculated on the basis of his age and physical condition. The weapon with which he was provided was a short sword, the *gladio*, hence the name gladiator. If he survived and showed strength, he could be awarded his freedom from slavery.

Trajan, Marcus Ulpius (53-117).

He defeated the Dacians in the campaigns of 101-103 and 107-108, and organised harsh persecutions against Christians guilty of denying the cult of Emperor-worship established by state law. His impressive building activity changed the appearance of the capital. The most famous constructions, of which important ruins remain, are Trajan's Forum with Trajan's Markets, the Libraries, Trajan's Column and Trajan's Temple.

Capitoline Museums, Emperors' Room. Trajan.

Trajan's Column. (detail).

Trajan's Forum, Trajan's Column

Location of the monuments.
1) Trajan's Forum.
2) Trajan's Markets.
3) Trajan's Column..

Trajan's Forum. The Forum, located in an area near the slopes of the Quirinal Hill, was planned by Apollodorus of Damascus and executed between 107 and 112. It included a temple, two libraries, the basilica, the column, the markets and the equestrian statue of Trajan. Entry was from the adjoining Forum of Augustus.

Trajan's Column. Rising 40 metres, the column was erected to celebrate the campaign against the Dacians, and disposed as a mausoleum to hold the ashes of the emperor and his family. The shaft and reliefs of this work of art have remained intact, though the gilding has disappeared. The sculptures describe the work of the legionaries: the building of the bridge over the Danube, crossing rivers, assaults and conquests of entrenched camps, the capture and execution of prisoners. The legionaries move with realistic gestures, expressions and movements. The figures and landscapes are set on different planes to give

prominence to the figures, isolated or in groups, to the forest landscapes and to the walls of besieged forts.

Trajan's Markets. The planning and execution of Trajan's Markets, which implied levelling the rise between the Capitol

Trajan's Forum, Trajan's Markets.

Trajan's Forum. Trajan's Column (detail).

connected with stairs from the level of the forum to the upper storeys where the office quarters were located. Apollodoro of Damascus, the architect in charge of the work, drew up the plan setting aside space for roads, the loading and unloading of merchandise, access to office quarters, internal links between storeys, and water canalisation. The exedra of the construction visible from the open space of the Forum shows us the division into three levels, with windows in correspondence with shops and workshops, distinguished by different architectural styles according to the merchandise on sale or to the particular use of the premises. Via Biberatica, which handled a greater movement of people, was framed by shops specialising in the sale of spices. The marble that embellished the interior, which leads us to presume that they were patronized by an exclusive clientele, has now vanished.

The **Forum of Nerva or Transitorio** is a work by the architect Rabirio. This Forum, also called "Foro Transitorio", communicated with the Suburra, the ill-famed quarter of Rome, through the Argiletum. The very large temple dedicated to Minerva was the most conspicuous.

and the Quirinal and the construction of a large trading area made up of shops, offices, meeting and negotiation halls appeared from the very start a very demanding job. The architectural complex was crossed East to West by via Biberatica,

Publius Aelius Hadrianus (76-138).

During the first period after his election he followed in his predecessor's footsteps. However he soon realised the futility of war and turned to visiting various provinces of the Empire especially Greece and Egypt, and began the construction of grandiose works to modernise the city. In Jerusalem, he had a temple built in honour of Jupiter on the ruins of the Temple of Jahweh; In Rome, he built Hadrian's Tomb and the Temple to Venus and Rome; in Tivoli, Hadrian's Villa and in Britannia, Hadrian's Wall. Hadrian's period is considered the golden age of the Empire.

Capitoline Museums, Emperors' Room. Hadrian.

Pantheon, façade.

The Elephant of Minerva (detail).

The **Pantheon** was built under Agrippa in 27 B.C. and dedicated to Mars and Venus, protectors of the Gens Julia. In 80 A.D., following damage caused by a fire, the Emperor Hadrian had it rebuilt. The plan was laid out in accordance with the technical and functional wishes of the emperor in person, and the result, despite the 1,800 years that have passed, can still be seen today. The magnificent round hall, covered by a dome with a diameter of 44 metres with an oculus of 9, rises from the ground to 44 metres. The supporting wall in a cylindrical shape that is 6 metres thick rises 22 metres and is formed by two walls separated by an interstice. The cylinder brings out the geometrical form of the sphere, while that of a pyramid, which is projected by the base platform up to the central oculus can be identified on the sides of the equilateral triangles. In the Pantheon these geometrical figures – circle, pyramid and sphere – lend substance to the theory of Pythagoras, the philosopher who considered numbers and geometrical figures as fundamental elements in the architecture of the entire universe. Hadrian was an enthusiastic follower of Pythagoras and his theories. In the lower part

the walls hollow out into seven niches, each decorated with columns and pilasters, while the one at the end is arched. In the upper part of the immense sphere are the trabeation, attic (once embellished with rare marble), and the lacunar vaults that narrow as they approach the oculus. In this stimulating space, which geometry cleansed of its impurities, the Emperor Hadrian dominated, dispensing justice to the inhabitants of the immense Roman Empire.

Pantheon, interior.

Pantheon, vault.

Tivoli, Hadrian's Villa.

Castel Sant'Angelo or Hadrian's Tomb.

Hadrian's Villa (125-134). The Emperor Hadrian had long planned to build an urban complex in which he would be able to carry out his functions as Emperor and Pontifex Maximus. He decided to choose a suitable location on the slopes of Tivoli, far enough from Rome to feel completely free but not too distant from the city. The project materialised in the construction of a series of rooms and adaptation of areas, indoor and outdoor, suitable for carrying out a specific function. The seemingly obscure names given to each of them reminded the Emperor of what he had seen in Greece and in Egypt. The buildings were called Poecile, Nymphaeum or Maritime Theatre, Baths, Canopus, Museum, Imperial Palace, Terrace of Tempe, Academy. The Poecile was a rectangular portico and recalled the one in Athens. The Nymphaeum or Maritime Theatre was a circular building composed of a group of concentric structures and a central small temple with half-dome and throne. The small temple, surrounded by water, could be reached by passing over footbridges on wheels that, if removed, isolated it. The Canopus was a long basin that terminated at the sanctuary of Serapis, its sides embellished with columns and statues. The sanctuary or Serapis, in the shape of a nymph, had an exedra with concentric basins where water descended to form delightful little waterfalls. The statues of Isis, Osiris and of Egyptian gods ennobled it.

Hadrian's Tomb, today Castel Sant'Angelo, was built by the Emperor Hadrian between 135 and 139 to serve as a mausoleum for himself, his family and the members of his court. The complex had a square base, surmounted by a cylindrical main part and a mound of earth with pine trees. On the top a chariot with the figure of the Emperor and the symbols of Helios or the Sun stand out. Inside were the basement, where the urns with ashes were kept, the spiral ramp and the gallery. Outside, the Helios Bridge, built over the river, connected the Tomb

Temple of Venus and Rome.

to the city. Aurelian, in 271, transformed the structure into a defence bastion, later used as a prison until the 20th century. What remains of the original building are the square wall with bastions, the cylindrical main part and the terrace. The interior contains rooms of different periods. The Roman Hall of Justice, the Room of Apollo restored in 1547 by Pope Paul III, the Chapel of Pope Leo X, the apartments of Pope Clement VII, the courtyard of Pope Alexander VI, the Loggia of Pope Paul III, the Loggia of Pope Julius II facing the Helios Bridge, the apartment of Pope Paul III with the Rooms of the Council, of Perseus, Love and Psyche, the latter decorated with frescoes by Perin del Vaga and Baccio da Montelupo, the Library Room and the Treasury Room from the Roman period, which even today contains coffers.

Little soul, wandering, pleasant, guest and companion of my body, which now departs into places, pale, rigid, bare, you will no longer give jokes.

Hadrian's farewell

Temple of Venus and Rome (Hadrian, 121-136). It was a building made up of two cellas, united in the apses with enormous statues portraying the divinities. The architect Apollodorus of Damascus, who was given the project, refused to accept statues tall enough to go through the roof and expressed his resentment to the Emperor himself. The Emperor, on the contrary, wanted to make the concept of divinity stand out, so that the parameters applied by mortals had no value: Apollodorus lost his life. This temple of Venus and Rome had a roof covered with flat gold tiles, which in the 7th century were removed and adapted to cover the roof of the ancient St. Peter's Basilica. The ruins of the Temple of Venus and Rome are in front of the Colosseum.

Marcus Aurelius Antoninus (121-180)

He won the war against the Parthians (161-166) and against the Germans, successes that conferred him his triumph. Elected Emperor, the dismal state of public finances forced him to impose heavy taxation, which jeopardised the popularity he enjoyed. He was a follower of Stoic philosophy. He had the column erected in Piazza Colonna as well as the equestrian statue, still standing today because it is believed to be of Constantine.

Capitoline Museums, Emperors' Room. Marcus Aurelius.

Equestrian statue of Marcus Aurelius, Capitol Stairway (partial view), Statue of the Dioscuri, Palazzo Nuovo (partial view), Façade of Santa Maria in Aracoeli (partial view), Vittoriano (partial view).

Location of the monuments.
1) Piazza del Campidoglio
2) Piazza Colonna.

Piazza del Campidoglio, designed by Michelangelo, is laid out in an inverted trapezium framed by buildings. At the time of ancient Rome the façade of the buildings on the Capitol faced the Forum, the centre of the city. During the centuries that followed the fall of the Empire and during the Middle Ages, the Forum was abandoned and covered with debris. Grass grew over it and it became pastureland, the monuments were destroyed and the stones used for construction. In his plan for the Piazza, Michelangelo took the needs of the new layout for the city into account and turned the buildings towards Campo Marzio. The **Column of Marcus Aurelius** is in Piazza Colonna. In the days of ancient Rome, this area corresponded to Campus Martius. The Column was built between 176 and 193 in honour of Marcus Aurelius for his victories over the Marcomanni, the Quadis and the Sarmatians. With a height of 29.6 m and a diameter of 3.7 m, the bas-reliefs depict the German and Sarmatian wars.

Diocletian, Gaius Aurelius Valerius *(245-313)*

Because of the increasing difficulties and continuing barbarian invasions over the borders, the Emperor Diocletian decided to associate Maximianus Gaius Galerius and Flavius Constantius, in the government assigning to each of them the seats of Nicomedia, Sirmium, Milan, and Trier, as capitals of the territories to be administered. He had an entrenched camp built for thousands of kilometres to defend the borders and constructed roads, gardens and houses in Rome. His most remarkable work were the Baths that are named after him.

Capitoline Museums, Emperors' Room. Diocletian.

BATHS OF DIOCLETIAN

Baths of Diocletian and Piazza Esedra.
Baths of Diocletian, National Museum of Rome.

The construction of the Baths was started by Maximianus in 298 and terminated by Diocletian in 305. It covered a large area that now stretches from the National Museum of Rome or the Museum of the Baths, from Piazza della Repubblica to the Basilica of Santa Maria degli Angeli, to the Certosa Cloister. In the 16th century

National Museum of Rome, Ludovisi Throne. Aphrodite.

Michelangelo was made responsible for renovating the internal and external areas. Displayed in some interiors, important works make up the National Museum of Rome. Among these are several masterpieces. The Dying Galatian commiting suicide with his wife, a replica of a bronze sculpture dedicated to King Attalus I, conqueror of the Galatians, dated to approximately the middle of the 3rd century B.C. The Ludovisi Throne is an exquisite relief of two nymphs, symbols of Sacred and Profane Love and of Venus, the goddess of love, rising from the sea foam. An original work of the 5th century B.C. is the Head of a Goddess, an Erinys with hair clinging to her head. In the Cloister: Ares Ludovisi, with a dreamy expression, the Apollo of the Tiber, the Discus Thrower of Castelporziano; the Niobidae, a nude of the 4th century B.C. from the Gardens of Sallust; the Venus of Cyrene; the ephebus of Subiaco, recovered from Nero's Villa; the Resting Boxer, and the Girl of Anzio. The Augustus of Via Labicana is shown carrying out the function of Pontifex Maximus. On the first floor: the frescoes that decorated the hall of the Villa of Livia, wife of Augustus, at Prima Porta.

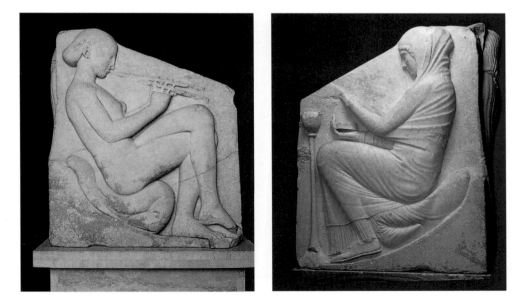

Constantine the Great *(280-337)*

During the decisive years in the struggle for power, Constantine sided with the Christians, who had become prominent in number and importance. Elected emperor, he provided Christianity with enormous wealth. He later ceded power to the Bishop of Rome and moved to Byzantium, where he established the capital of the Empire taking numerous works of art with him.

Capitoline Museums, Emperors' Room. Constantine.

Basilica of Maxentius and Constantine.

In his public and private life, Constantine lived the transition from the pagan to the Christian world. The leading figures of this transformation that took place over several centuries were the Christians, who counted among their ranks nobles, members of the equestrian order, Roman merchants and all the populations that lived on the shores of the Mediterranean and in Europe. The Christians and Byzantines brought laws and civilisation, while the Barbarians originating from the north-eastern forests of the continent were incited to conquer the lands where civilisation flourished. The change was first enacted with the Edicts of Constantine of 313 and 330, in which the supremacy of Christianity over other religions was officially recognised both from the spiritual and material point of view.

Arch of Constantine

Arch of Constantine (detail).

The **Basilica of Maxentius and Constantine** was built between 306 and 312 as the seat of the Courts and trade bargaining. It had the shape of a rectangle with columns of rare beauty, one of which can be seen in Piazza Santa Maria Maggiore. The statue of Constantine, of which several enormous pieces remain, reminiscent of the Colossus of Nero, convey an idea of the importance and consideration in which the emperor was held.

The **Arch of Constantine,** built between 312 and 315 to celebrate the victory over Maxentius and the affirmation of the power of the new emperor, is an arch with three barrel vaults. Dating from the Roman period, it has jealously been preserved by the Church over the centuries. The bas-reliefs that adorn it have a dual function and are of different origins. The panels with moulded scenes that were taken from the monuments of Trajan, Hadrian and Marcus Aurelius are fine works in the best of Roman tradition. The sculptures of the other panels, artistically speaking, do not surpass the provincial ambit: the Siege of Verona, the Battle of the Milvian Bridge, and the Emperor entering Rome and, in another, the Emperor speaking to the people.

FROM PAGANISM TO CHRISTIANITY

The ancient Appian Way.

Portico of Octavia.

Catacombs of St. Pancras.

Rome at the time of Constantine (306-337). With a population of one million inhabitants, it had two circles of walls, 190 granaries, 250 mills, two general markets, eleven aqueducts, eleven forums, eleven baths, ten basilicas, 36 arches, 1,150 fountains, 28 libraries, two circuses, and two amphitheatres. It was divided into quarters, adorned with luxurious gardens and had paved roads. The life of the inhabitants was regulated by Imperial decrees, in use from the time of the Emperor Augustus, and enforced by guards. Traders, money changers and lawyers were active in the forums; merchandise and passengers arrived and left from the port; goods on display outside shops blocked the roads; the echo of brawls could be heard from Suburra, the working-class quarter and sometimes the glimmer of fires could be seen in the distance. At night the city became dangerous, chariots raced through the streets, rubbish was thrown from windows and bands of delinquents would often steal and plunder.

The invasions and Christianity. The barbarians coming from the North were driven by hunger and the desire of conquest. Slaves, serfs and soldiery assaulted cities, hiding in the abandoned forests and countryside subject to floods. These hordes led to the disintegration of any form of the State, destroying it in the chaos of the 6th, 7th, and 8th centuries. However, temples, libraries, palace collections, and monuments remained open and henceforth they were plundered in Rome, the territories of the peninsula and the Empire. Christianity took over Roman buildings transforming them into basilicas and churches, also building monasteries and preserving as much as possible of the ancient codices. Above all Christianity preached the word of equality and love, imposing itself forcefully in relations between individuals and peoples.

The Appian Way is the most famous road of ancient Rome: opened in 312 B. C. by Appius Claudius and later extended as far as Brindisi, it became the line of direct communication with the Orient. It was the busiest route for the transit of legions and merchandise. Paved with thick slabs of basalt and in some places, just outside the walls of Rome, it had sidewalks. In respect of the laws

Spanish Steps.

issued by the Senate to avoid the outbreak of plague that had decimated the population many times, tombs had to be built outside the city walls. The Appian Way thus became the designated area for tombs and mausoleums, both of which were decorated with a statue of the deceased and a description of his praiseworthy deeds. The Appian Way slopes downwards in a setting of pine trees and aqueducts and its atmosphere recalls the history, films and theatres that have made it popular and the villas, more or less hidden, bring historical periods alive.

The **Church of Quo Vadis** was built on the place where Christ appeared to Peter, who was abandoning Rome to escape execution. Christ spoke to him with these words: "Peter, where are you going? Quo Vadis?" and Peter turned back in sacrifice.

Church of Santa Prassede. The Chapel of St. Zeno (Pope Paschal I, 9th century) with the series of mosaics. Church of Santa Pudenziana. Mosaic in the apse (4th century) and others from the 11th century.

Basilica of St. Clement. The upper construction, dating from the 12th century, has been restored; the lower part dates from the 4th century. The interior contains decorations of the primitive church: *schola cantorum*, ambo, candelabrum for the Easter candle, and the ciborium that protects the remains of St. Clement. The Triumph of the Cross (mosaic, 12th century); Chapel of Santa Caterina with frescoes by Masolino da Panicale (1431). Lower construction: frescoes (11th – 12th century).

Church of Stefano Rotondo (5th century), Roman style building with ancient columns. Church of Santi Giovanni e Paolo (5th century).

Porta San Paolo (4th century) with the Pyramid of Caius Cestius and sepulchral cell (12 B. C.). The Protestant Cemetery, where Percy Bysshe Shelley and John Keats are also buried. The Testaccio, the mountain built with broken amphorae, renowned for the games and popular feasts. Via della Marmorata where, in Roman times, marble was unloaded. On the Aventine Hill: Church of Santa Sabina, with carved doors dating from the 5th century, Sant' Alessio, Santa Prisca.

Tiberina Island.

Quirinal Palace.

Baths of Caracalla.

Basilica of St. John Lateran.

Basilica of St. Paul's Outside the Walls.

THE BASILICAS

The ancient basilica was a square building, divided into naves by columns and flanked by colonnades that opened towards the interior and the road. It was the seat of the court of justice and shops were located in the rooms along the walls and in the interior of the porticos. Some private buildings with sufficient space had an internal room, with columns and apses, where meetings were held. Until the first half of the 4th century, when their religion was considered a threat for imperial institutions, Christians secretly met in these private rooms.

The **Lateran** took its name from an ancient Roman property, whose buildings had been confiscated by Nero and donated several centuries later by Constantine to Pope Melchiades, who began development of the area until it became the centre of Christianity.

The **Basilica of St. John Lateran**, which boasts an ancient tradition and was the venue for remarkable events, was built by Borromini in 1646 under Pope Innocent X. Its façade was redone by Alessandro Galilei in 1735. The statues of the façade and the cloister are remarkable. Mosaics dating from the fifth century can be

Basilica of Santa Maria Maggiore.

Church of Santa Maria Cosmedin.

viewed in the fourth-century baptistery. The stairway is dated 380. The popes' Crypt is from the 3rd century. It is worth remembering the other two basilicas that go back to the beginnings of the rise of Christianity: the Basilica of St. Paul and the Basilica of St. Lawrence.

Basilica of Santa Maria Maggiore. The original building, on the Esquiline Hill goes back to the 5th century. The present-day building has two façades: the first one with a portico, where the statue of Philip IV, King of Spain is set, and the eighteenth-century loggia by F. Fuga and the thirteenth-century mosaics of A. Rusuti can be seen. The second is the work of three architects: F. Ponzio, C. Rainaldi, and D. Fontana. The Baroque style interior has an area of 86 metres divided by 40 columns into a nave and two aisles. The mosaic panels date from the 5th century, the arch of triumph from the 5th century and the mosaic in the apse, by J. Torriti, from the 13th century.

The **Church of Santa Maria Cosmedin** 4th century, is a transformed building. The church is near the Theatre of Marcellus in Piazza della Bocca della Verità which corresponds to Rome's ancient Forum Boarium.

THE VATICAN CITY

THE RENAISSANCE POPES

Statue of St. Peter.

St. Peter's Basilica at night.

The period of the Renaissance popes (last quarter of the 15th century, first half of the 16th century) can be compared to the golden age of the Roman Emperors. In ancient Rome, the descendants of a gens received a Humanist education in Athens and Alexandria. On their return they brought with them works of art and were accompanied by famous artists, the ambassadors of the way of life of those societies. Palazzi and villas embellished the city. In a relatively short time, Rome changed appearance and began to have a special attraction for artists and traders.

During the Middle Ages, in tragic periods of history, the Popes had assumed a limitless moral power. This represented a strong attraction for the population, which turned to the Bishop of Rome not only for spiritual salvation but also to ensure their worldly survival.

In the 15th century, following the example of the Medici in Florence, so important for culture and the arts, the Vatican became the promoter in Rome of a strong artistic movement. This attracted the best Florentine artists and men of letters, who created works that remain unequalled in architecture, sculpture, painting and in the letters.

By following past tradition and avoiding identification as head of an army - with the exception of Julius II - Sixtus IV, Leo X, Clement VII, and Urban VIII interfered in the affairs of other states, influencing their politics and supporting their culture and arts. When the Lutheran movement appeared to be menacing Church doctrine, the Popes approved the Jesuit Order, which defended it by erecting an insurmountable wall against any attempt to corrode the pillars of its doctrine.

Sixtus IV, Francesco della Rovere (1471-1484). Favouring the affluence of family and friends, he fomented the Pazzi conspiracy with the intention of obtaining the Duchy of Florence. When the plan failed, he excommunicated the city. He celebrated the Jubilee Year in 1475. He connected Castel Sant'Angelo to St. Peter's with a long passageway (Passetto), and built the Sistine Chapel.

Julius II, Giuliano della Rovere (1503-1513). He harshly criticised the political activity and way of life of Alexander VI, and before being elected Pope he abandoned Rome to avoid becoming involved in the intrigue of the Papal Court. His strong influence in European politics led to the formation of the League of Cambrai. He participated in the construction of the Cathedral of Orvieto.

Leo X, Giovanni de' Medici (1513-1521). Son of Lorenzo the Magnificent and Clarice Orsini, he received a princely education, and travelled throughout Europe where he met the most influential political and economic figures. When he returned to Rome his palazzo became a meeting place for artists and men of letters. Elected Pope, his policies concentrated on the return of the Medici to Florence and on strengthening the power of the Church.

Clement VII, Giulio de' Medici (1523-1534). He lived at the court of his uncle, Leo X. As a result of his political intrigues, he witnessed the Sack of Rome in 1527. In promoting the arts he turned to artists with the calibre of Michelangelo and Raphael.

Urban VIII, Maffeo Barberini (1623-1644). With his political actions and the renewal of the customs of the Papal Court, he tried to consolidate the prestige of the Church. With the help of the Jesuits he had Galileo and Campanella put on trial. He contributed to the improvement of Rome's city plan by building fountains, palazzi and gardens and by widening the roads.

The Cathedra.

*Michelangelo's Dome
from the interior of the Basilica.*

Sixtus IV, Francesco della Rovere *(1471-1484)*

The prototype of the Renaissance pope, he reformed the Church, approved the Inquisition, and upheld Torquemada. He was a patron of the arts, enriching the Vatican Library by recovering manuscripts and books from Europe and the Middle East. He had the Sistine Chapel built by Baccio Pontelli on a plan similar to the temple destroyed in Jerusalem.

Vatican Museums. Sixtus IV.

St. Peter's Basilica. Façade.
Swiss Guards.

The **Vatican City** is located on the right bank of the Tiber River in the area of the old Vatican zone, which gave it its name and where, in ancient Romans times, Nero's Gardens and the Circus stood. The borders of this city-state are, on the west, the fortifications of Pope Leo IV,

St. Peter's Square and Basilica.

built in 847; on the north, south and east, the Passetto with Castel Sant'Angelo and the Borghi. Extending along the central axis of the east side, in addition to the Basilica and St. Peter's Square, is Via della Conciliazione, flanked by buildings and gardens, squares and roads that make up a vast urban complex where the services of the Vatican State are located. St. Peter's Basilica and Square are part of the Vatican City and constitute the centre of the Roman Catholic Church.

St. Peter's Square (340 x 240 m) was designed and executed by G. L. Bernini from 1656 to 1667, under Pope Alexander VII. The area, surrounded by 284 columns, 88 pilasters and decorated with 140 statues, widens in the centre to form two hemicycles. During the period of Pope Paul V, Gian Lorenzo Bernini built the fountain on the left and C. Maderno the one on the right. The Obelisk in the centre, 25.5 metres high, was brought from Heliopolis in Egypt in 37 A.D. under Emperor Caligula, and placed in the Circus of Nero. Several old prints show it, in the Middle Ages, beside the ancient St. Peter's Basilica. It is said that Caesar's ashes were kept above in the spire at the time of the Romans where a relic of the Holy Cross now lies. Under Pope Sixtus V, the obelisk

was raised in four months by the architect C. Fontana with 44 hoists, the work of 900 workers and the strength of 140 horses. It is an ancient decorative element that gives depth and co-ordinates the various points of the square, which is considered a masterpiece of the Baroque style.

St. Peter's Basilica stands on the area of Nero's Circus, where St. Peter suffered martyrdom and was buried. The Greek cross plan of the building, designed in the 15th century by the architect Bramante, was at first modified by Michelangelo and then transformed into a Latin cross by C. Maderno, who completed the façade in 1614, during the pontificate of Pope Paul V. In the central balcony, the Loggia delle Benedizioni, the newly elected pope is presented to the people in a symbolic confirmation of his election. On the crowning of the façade, statues, each 5,7 m. high, of the Redeemer, the Baptist and of the Apostles, symbols of the New Testament rise as testimony of a conception of life based on love. In the portico are the entrance doors, including the one of Death by Manzù, one with the panels of Filarete (1433-45) and the Holy Door that is opened and closed to mark the Jubilee Year. On pedestals are the statues of Constantine and Charlemagne.

Julius II, Giuliano della Rovere *(1503-1513)*

Nephew of Sixtus IV, he enforced the temporal power of the Church by engaging directly in acts of war. He conceded more freedom to the Jews, built St. Peter's Basilica, had frescoes done in the Rooms of the Signatura by Raphael and in the vault of the Sistine Chapel by Michelangelo, with the Creation.

Vatican Museums. Julius II.

St. Peter's Basilica. Interior.
Arnolfo di Cambio. Statue of St. Peter.

The interior is immense (186 m. long, the nave rises to 44 m; dome: diameter 42 m, height 136 m). The visitor should be left to become familiar with the space, observe the dome of Michelangelo from the transept, the statues and the decorations. Perhaps the notion that the passing centuries have left traces on every pillar will take hold. Next to the central doorway in the interior, a red porphyry disk can be seen, once in front of the great altar where the emperors knelt to receive the crown from the Pope. The middle nave is laid out like the churches of the Counter-Reformation, and from the niches opened between the pilasters, from 1706, large statues of the founders of the religious orders stand out. It is easy to find a few points of reference threading from ancient Rome up to the present day.

The **Pietà** by Michelangelo (1499-1500). The group of the Pietà, in Carrara marble, shaped like a pyramid, shows the Virgin Mother holding her dead son on her knees. From a technical point of view this work was composed by contrasts: the figures in a vertical and crosswise position, the bodies, one dressed one bare, and finally the illuminated face and the hidden hand. The anguish that the face expresses with its fixedness is transposed into a metaphysical feeling.

Michelangelo. The Pietà.

Statue of St. Peter. Arnolfo di Cambio created this statue in 1298 with the bronze obtained from the statue of Jupiter Capitoline that was in the Capitol. This bronze, once symbol of the Empire, now depicts Peter, the symbol of Christianity. The continuity of the pagan world with the Christian is also perceptible in the positioning of the head, in the drapery of the dress and in the humble and open pose of Peter. Visitors stop and stoop to kiss his foot, perhaps consuming it.

The **Baldachin**. 29 m high, was executed by Bernini between 1624 and 1633 with the bronze obtained from the beams of the Pantheon by order of Pope Urban VIII.

"Quod non fecerunt Barbari, fecerunt Barberini". (What the Barbarians did not do the Barberini did). The Romans had the occasion to read this epigram from the talking statue of Pasquino; it underscored the discontent, caused by the Barberini Pope, Urban VIII, for having destroyed the bronze beams of the Pantheon to make the Baldachin, which dominates in the centre of St. Peter's Basilica. The Baldachin protects the altar, at which the Pope alone may say Mass. The altar is situated above the Confession, where the relics of St. Peter are preserved. The marble statue of Pius VI, by Canova, is in front.

Pope Leo X, Giovanni de' Medici *(1513-1521)*

He kept away from Rome, visiting the courts of Europe during the pontificate of Alexander VI. When he returned to Rome, he took up residence in Palazzo Madama and surrounded himself with artists and men of letters. He was a skilful diplomat even though he underestimated the work of Luther and the decisions of Henry VIII. He contributed to the embellishment and transformation of Rome. His motto was "Hic manebimus optime".

Vatican Museums. Leo X.

G. L. Bernini, the Baldachin.

G. L. Bernini, the Cathedra.

The monument to Paolo III Farnese, by Della Porta (1551-75) represents the reclining statues of Justice, a portrait of his sister Giulia, of Prudence, and of his mother Giovannella Caetani. The third chapel, called Colonna, shows the altarpiece with San Leo meeting Attila (A. Algardi) and contains the sepulchres of Leo II, Leo III, Leo IV and Leo XII.

The **Cathedra** is located at the end of the apse. Bernini (1656-65), with this Chair, produced a symbolic work in Baroque style. The statues of Ambrose and Augustine, Athanasius and John Chrysostom, represent the pillars of Church doctrine. Within, another is preserved in wood where Peter is said to have sat.

The **Dome of Michelangelo** is remarkable for its size from the centre of the transept. It is sustained by four enormous pentagonal pillars with a perimeter of 71 metres. The structure is a double shell with stairs running through the space between. With a height of 132.5 metres and a diameter of 42, it is the most grandiose work of Michelangelo executed after having studied the dome of the Pantheon.

The **Sacristy.** It is a separate building of the 18th century. The list, carved in marble, of the 144 popes buried in the basilica can be seen at the entrance. In the common sacristy are the eight ancient grey columns, recovered from Villa Adriana; the bronze cock of the 4th century once on the campanile of the previous basilica is an evident allusion to the words of Christ to Peter "before the cock crows, you will have denied me three times". In the sacristy of the Beneficiati: the Ciborium of Donatello, 1432. The Treasury Room, in which the objects that escaped the last plunder sanctioned by the Treaty

of Tolentino of 1797 are kept, the richness and finishing of the vestments and the Ring of Sixtus IV; the Cross of the Emperor Justin II; the Dalmatic of the 10th or 11th century; the candelabra of Pollaiolo are astonishing. The Vatican Grottoes are located halfway between the present-day basilica and the one of Constantine. There are tombstones, the monument to Sixtus IV by Pollaiolo (1493), and a representative work of the early Renaissance. You can descend into the pagan-Christian necropolis over which the primitive basilica was built. The Old Grottoes. The tombstones, busts, and inscriptions that recall several popes buried in the previous basilica, such as Boniface VIII and Innocent VII are remarkable. The altar is of the 4th century. The New Grottoes (1534-46) offer several chapels and parts of the monument to Paul II (G. Dalmata and Mino da Fiesole, 1471), statues, and the fourth-century altar in the Chapel of St. Peter. In the exit wing is the sarcophagus of Giunio Basso of the 1st century.

Clement VII, Giulio de' Medici *(1523-1534).*

Son of Giuliano de' Medici, his pontificate took place during the period of the struggle between France and Spain for supremacy in Italy and was full of events that shook Europe in the field of religion and politics: King Henry VIII declared himself head of the Church of England, Martin Luther introduced Protestantism, and the Sack of Rome (1527) was one of the most disconcerting acts of barbarism against civilisation. Even the style of Michelangelo's Last Judgement brings us echoes of those events.

Vatican Museums. Clement VII.

St. Peter's Basilica. Dome of Michelangelo. Interior.

Urban VIII, Maffeo Barberini *(1623-1644).*

He attempted to give the Church the maximum prestige in Europe He brought Galileo and Campanella to trial. He stimulated architecture in Rome with the construction of fountains and palazzi.

Vatican Museums. Urban VIII.

The Apollo Belvedere.

The **Vatican Museums**. A visit to the museums is a source of unexpected surprises that can vary at any moment. The Gregorian Egyptian Museum; the Pigna Courtyard, dominated by the large niche of P. Ligorio and an enormous bronze pine cone from the Roman period; the Chiaramonti Museum, arranged according to the dictates of Antonio Canova, also includes the Lapidaria Gallery, a collection of pagan and Christian inscriptions; the Pio-Clementino Museum, with Greek and Roman sculptures including the Laocoon Group, the famous statue in Greek marble; the Gallery of Statues and the Room of the Muses, with the famous Belvedere Torso that inspired Michelangelo for the nudes of the Sistine Chapel.

Pio-Clementino Museum. The Laocoon is a group in marble from the 2nd century B.C. recovered in 1506 from Nero's Domus Aurea and signed by Agesander, Athenodoros and Polydorus of Rhodes. It represents three figures, one of a man, the priest Laocoon, which dominates the others of two young boys, his sons, taken together, as with superhuman force, they try to struggle free from the coils of giant snakes that are suffocating them. This mythological scene takes place in front of a door of the city of Troy, where the inhabitants surround a giant horse in animated discussion. The discussion revolves around whether to bring the horse inside the city walls, as the majority who consider it a gift from the gods would like to do, or set fire to it as sustained by the high priest who wants to destroy the horse, a presage of the city's ruin. The inhabitants prepare the fire as two enormous snakes reach Laocoon and his sons and suffocate them in their coils. Shaken by this miraculous scene, the inhabitants, convinced it was the wish of the gods, open the gate and push the horse inside the city. During the night the Greek warriors emerge and raze Troy, which they had not succeeded in taking by storm during the ten-year siege.

Apollo Belvedere. Roman copy of the 2nd century A.D. from a Greek original in bronze located in the Agora of Athens attributed to the sculptor Leochares (330-320 B. C.). The statue was discovered at the end of the 15th century. The Borgia Apartment was the residence of Pope Alexander VI, a setting that with regard to the people who stayed there, satisfies a certain amount of curiosity. The leading figures at the court of Pope Alexander VI, were Cesare Borgia, Lucrezia Borgia, Giulia Farnese, Vannozza, and Micheletto. Pinturicchio worked from 1492 to 1495 on the paintings decorating these rooms.

Raphael (1483-1520).

Born in Urbino, a town between Florence and Rome, he was influenced by these schools of painting. His smaller paintings are scattered among public and private collections around the world from Berlin to London, Lisbon and Paris as well as the United States. The frescoes remained at the Vatican. Raphael's paintings express the essence of Christianity.

Raphael Rooms, Signatura Room, The School of Athens.
Self-portrait of Raphael.

Pope Julius II, dissatisfied with the results achieved by the painters who were frescoing the rooms, called Raphael from Florence at Bramante's suggestion, and after evaluating a test, entrusted him with the task of decorating the rooms. The order of the frescoes is as follows: Signatura Room; Heliodorus Room, Room of the Fire in the Borgo, Constantine Room. Raphael reached his maximum artistic achievement in the Signatura Room, which he frescoed between 1508 and 1511.

The **Dispute of the Holy Sacrament** on the entrance wall. Three semicircles are enclosed in an area framed by an arch: above God the Father with Christ, the Virgin Mother and John the Baptist in the centre; on the sides, the Patriarchs and Prophets, Apostles and Confessors, symbols of the Old and New Testament. The central area is taken up by the Most Holy Sacrament surrounded by representatives of the religion, St. Gregory the Great, Savonarola, Beato Angelico, St. Jerome, St. Ambrose, St. Augustine, Dante and St. Thomas.

Triumph of Philosophy and the School of Athens (1509). The scene is set in a large space where the figures arranged individually or in groups have a point of reference in the two central figures: Plato, with the features of Leonardo da Vinci holding the Timaeus; Aristotle, looking downward, holds the book of Ethics. The other philosophers that take up the space reveal their identity by their posture: Diogenes lying down half-dressed, Heraclitus, with the features of Michelangelo, seated holding his head in his hand; Socrates intent on counting syllogisms; followed by all the others. Francesco Maria della Rovere, dressed in a white cloak, can be seen behind Anaxagoras; on the opposite side is the portrait of Raphael.

Glorification of Poetry, the Parnassus (1511). Apollo is playing the lyre and creates a melody that fascinates muses and poets. Homer, Virgil, Ennius, Sappho, Ariosto and Ovid express their full participation by the faraway look on their faces. Calliope, the muse closest to the god is portrayed with the greatest care and the figure's attraction is due to its almost abstract beauty. The figures of the court and Roman aristocracy fascinated by the art of this painter vied with each other to obtain a painting. Raphael, driven by the desire for bigger profits, did his utmost to satisfy the requests and his interest waned for the frescoes in the Vatican rooms. His apprentices Giulio Romano, F. Penni and Giovanni da Udine continued work in the Rooms on designs by Raphael. The frescoes of the Heliodorus Room, carried out from 1512 to 1514, illustrate the period of transition from the pontificate of Pope Julius II to that of Leo X. The portraits of Julius II and Raphael, and of Leo X, who as Leo the Great defeats Attila, are of great artistic value.

The **Loggias** were designed by Bramante and by Raphael himself from 1512 to 1518. *Grotesques* were used here for the first time.

Raphael Rooms, Signatura Room. School of Athens.

NEMO · SIBI · ASSV
AT · HONORE M ·
VOCATVS · AD
TANQVAM · AR

Sistine Chapel. Wall frescoes. The frescoes on the left wall were painted under Pope Sixtus IV from 1481 to 1483, with episodes from the life of Moses, the prophet of the Old Testament; on the right wall are paintings from the life of Jesus, which begins the New Testament. Moses in Egypt (Pinturicchio); Moses and the daughters of Jethro (Botticelli); Crossing of the Red Sea and Moses and the Tablets, by C. Rosselli; The Punishment of Korah by Botticelli, with a view of the Arch of Constantine and the Septizonium; The Death of Moses by Luca Signorelli, from which Michelangelo probably drew inspiration for the Nudes he painted on the vault. On the right wall: Baptism of Jesus by Pinturicchio; Temptation of Christ by Botticelli; the Calling of the Apostles by D. Ghirlandaio; Sermon on the Mount by C. Rosselli and Piero di Cosimo; Christ giving the Keys to St. Peter by Perugino and the Last Supper by C. Rosselli.

(128-129) Raphael Rooms,
Signature Room.
The Dispute of the Holy Sacrament
Sistine Chapel. Sandro Botticelli,
The Punishment of Korah, Dathan and Abiran.
(132-133) Sistine Chapel. Sandro Botticelli,
The Temptation of Christ.

Michelangelo Buonarroti *(1475-1564).*

Michelangelo himself described the tremendous effort it cost him to paint the ceiling of the Sistine Chapel: "Face dribbled--see?-- like a Byzantine floor, mosaic. From all this straining my guts and my hambones tangle, pretty near. Thank God I can swivel my butt about for ballast. Feet are out of sight; they just scuffle around, erratic. Up front my hide's tight elastic; in the rear it's slack and droopy, except where crimps have callused"

Florence, Academy Gallery. Daniele da Volterra, bust of Michelangelo.

The "Original Sin" is a scene that strikes the visitor: the painter's anguish in emphasising the thin line that separates the material from the spiritual world can be noticed. An unreal tree of life, unfinished, rises robust. Coiled firmly around the tree, the snake, assumes the figure of a young man, who bends his body and stretches out his arm offering Adam and Eve the satisfaction of their original pleasures. The head, arm, and body of Adam and Eve emanate the thrill of life that is taking place: at that very moment the Angel expels them pushing them towards life.

Michelangelo, view of the vault. The Expulsion from the Garden of Eden.

SISTINE CHAPEL

VAULT

Michelangelo
The Creation

Between 1508 and 1512, Michelangelo frescoed the vault of the Sistine Chapel, an area covering 800 metres: this was an arduos venture that made him explode from time to time with angry actions and words. In the central part there are several scenes illustrating the creation of the world: *The Drunkenness of Noah and The Flood; The Sacrifice of Noah, The Temptation and the Expulsion from Eden; The Creation of Adam and Eve,* which is undoubtedly the most well-known fresco. The figure of Adam emanates a primordial sense of weariness, almost as if the infusion of life is drawing him from a metaphysical distance. *The Separation of the Earth from Water; The Creation of fish, the sun, the moon, plants, The Separation of Light and Dark.* Figures of nudes are frescoed in the external corners of each panel, with the Sibyls and Prophets set below them. The Delphic Sybil and the Prophet Jeremiah are noteworthy above all for their spiritual intensity and character identification.

SISTINE CHAPEL

THE LAST JUDGEMENT

The Last Judgement
by Michelangelo

The Last Judgement, frescoed by Michelangelo by order of Paul III (1534-1541), is the expression of an apocalyptic event in which humanity is the desperate protagonist. The painter arrived in Rome during the pontificate of Pope Alexander VI, living experiences that had a profound effect on his soul. The fresco of the Last Judgement by Michelangelo is filled with the atmosphere of the first half of the 16th Cent. He centres the composition of the immense fresco on the figure of Christ and treats the theme of the Last Judgement along the dividing line between the natural and the supernatural. The contours of his powerful figure are natural, but are purposely muted by the shadow of the hand and arm driven to give judgement as a symbol of a supernatural act to which humanity must submit. The Virgin Mother turns inwards as if to protect herself, even though she participates in the action of God the Son without hope. Humanity with its variety of persons shows only vice and virtue: those on the right, risen again to a new life, and those on the left that precipitate, dragged down by the devils of their materialness.

Capitolium. Façade.

ANCIENT OSTIA

Ostia was the trading centre of the Roman Empire during the early years of its expansion, a port from which ships sailed towards lands then unknown and a centre for the distribution of foodstuffs destined for Rome. Ostia is considered the first Roman colony: tradition has it that it was founded by the King Ancus Martius, at the place where Aeneas landed. In reality, the oldest nucleus of the city, the castrum, can be dated to the 4th century B.C. and it was surrounded by walls with sixteen doors, four on each side, and crossed by two main roads set at a right angle to each other, the *decumanus maximus* - which was the east-west axis - and the *cardo maximus*, on the north-south axis. The Capitolium was the most important temple of Ostia. Built by Hadrian over the ruins of a pre-existing temple in brick, later covered with marble, Jupiter, Juno and Minerva were worshipped here. Opposite the Capitolium is the Temple of Rome and Augustus, dating from the Julio-Claudian period, and next to it are the Baths of the Forum, the largest in Ostia, built in the 2nd century. The dwellings have preserved mosaics and paintings.

House of the Charioteers.

Baths of the Seven Sages.

TIVOLI

Villa d'Este. based on a plan by Pirro Ligorio, Ippolito d'Este, Cardinal of Ferrara, son of Lucrezia Borgia and Alfonso I d'Este, built it in 1550. The most important interiors are the Room of Cardinals, the Room of the Arts and Crafts, the Room of Hercules, and the Throne Room. The latter opens onto a panoramic terrace. The Villa owes its fame to the magnificent Italian gardens full of fountains and statues, and century-old trees and ornamental plants. To implement his plan, Ligorio had an underground gallery of over 500 metres long excavated to carry water from the Aniene River into the basins of the Villa to supply the 250 waterspouts, the waterfalls and the 60 pools of water that fill the garden. The main fountains are the Organ Fountain and the Dragon Fountain, designed by Tommaso da Siena, though the Ovato Fountain is perhaps the most beautiful. The Avenue of the Hundred Fountains is 100 metres long. The Bicchierone Fountain is attributed to Bernini.

ROYAL PALACE OF CASERTA

It was built by L. Vanvitelli between 1752-1774 for the Bourbon king, Charles III. The plan is rectangular, the main façade has 243 windows, and the entire complex has 1,200 rooms.

Villa d'Este, Ovato Fountain.

Royal Palace. Façade, entrance.

Royal Palace. Park, waterfalls.

Royal Palace. Interior

Naples

Nowadays, for the tourist visiting Naples for the first time, the city is surprising and bewildering. It is impossible to understand its character and peculiar aspects merely with a quick tour as the structure of the city is so complex, the appearance of the monuments, buildings and layout of the town so full of contrasts, the scenery around the city so varied, and the people and their way of life so surprising. And yet the character of the city and its particular way of being are the sum of all these aspects, which are so

Naples. View of the Bay

complex, contradictory and chaotic and yet so forcefully alive. The street is indeed a theatre, the stage where actors play out their role in the scenario of everyday life, with popular festivals, grand processions, illuminations and fireworks. Popular festivals like the Santa Maria del Carmine Festival on 16 July, with the final spectacular fire set to the bell tower of the church, or the Piedigrotta Festival on 8 September at the Municipal Gardens, with its virtuoso performances in the art of illumination are likewise a dramatic backdrop. The grand processions and religious festivals - like the one of St. Januarius on 19 September, when all of Naples flocks around the Cathedral for a special ceremony in which the crowd is both spectator and player, waiting in expectation to follow every phase of the miracle of St. Januarius - are theatre. The churches adorned for wedding ceremonies, with a profusion of velvet, silk, ribbons, carpets and flowers, for which experts in the art of decoration are called, are theatre.

View of the Castel Nuovo area.

Royal Palace.

Neapolis was founded in the 6th century B.C. by Greek settlers in the area between present-day Via Foria and Santa Maria di Costantinopoli, Corso Umberto I and Via Colletta. The settlement was crossed by three thoroughfares (decumani) intersected by minor roads (cardines), the plan of which is still intact today. Founded by a population with a highly developed civilisation, the city flourished for a long period and succeeded in maintaining its independence even after the arrival of the Romans on the shores of the Gulf. Rome's loyal ally in the struggles against Pyrrhus and

Hannibal, Neapolis retained the Greek language and institutions, a fact that was not only tolerated, but even favoured by the Romans who, notoriously fascinated by Greek culture, found in the nearby city the ideal place for studies and pleasure.

After the fall of the Roman Empire, there was a short period of changing fortunes during which Naples was conquered and lost several times by the Goths against the Byzantines. The latter regained possession in the middle of the sixth century. Besides, Byzantium, concerned by the Longobard ex-

Capri. I faraglioni.

Capri. La piazzetta.

Galleria Umberto I.

Naples. Palazzo Donn'Anna.

pansion into southern Italy, favoured the autonomy and development of a military state in Naples to counter the threat of the Longobards. In the year 661 Emperor Constans II nominated the first duke. This marked the beginning of the Duchy of Naples that, following other events a century later, would gain complete independence from Byzantium, successfully preserving it until the middle of the twelfth century. The Duchy was unable to resist the pressure of the Normans. Norman-Swabian domination (1140-1266) was an unfortunate period in the history of Naples. With the advent of the Angevin dynasty (1266), Naples regained its role as capital of the kingdom. The absence of a local culture fostered acceptance of the forms and traditions of the French Gothic style that we can find today in the churches of Santa Chiara, Sant' Eligio, Donnaregina and in the apse of San Lorenzo Maggiore. Nevertheless, the renovation of buildings was not paralleled by sufficient expansion of the city, giving rise to various problems that have now become macroscopic and are connected with the overcrowding of the old city centre, whose road system has remained that of the Greek city.

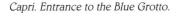

Positano.

Capri. Entrance to the Blue Grotto.

MASCHIO ANGIOINO

Castel Nuovo is popularly known as the Angevin Donjon (Maschio Angioino). Following his victory over the Swabians, Charles I of Anjou erected it near to the sea in order to defend and assert his rule. Work was planned and carried out between 1279-82. In the open area of Campus Oppidi rose the castle that was later called "new" to distinguish it from the older Castel dell'Ovo, Castel del Carmine and Castel Capuano. Though Charles himself never lived in the splendid castle, his successors resided there, and of course, churches, convents and noble palaces were naturally built

Sala Grande, the Vault.

around it. Piazza delle Correggie (so-called because of the jousts and tournaments held there) thus became an elegant and fashionable quarter where life in the capital was centred. The castle, ruined by the wars and sieges in the battle for succession in which the Durazzo Angevins and Angevin-Aragonese clashed, was rebuilt by Alfonso of Aragon in 1442. The splendid Triumphal Arch inserted between the two cylindrical towers (15th century) covered with trachyte tuff rightly rises as the symbol of Renaissance Naples. Many artists, not all of whom have been identified, devoted their work to this magnificent complex, whose design has been attributed by some to Sagrera and by others to Francesco Laurana.

The Sala Grande is also called Room of the Barons, after the day in 1486 when, with the pretext of summoning the barons for the wedding of one of his nieces, Ferrante imprisoned all the leaders of the conspiracy who were among the guests. It is a large square room with an octagonal vault, in which Sagrera transformed the architectural style into unusual and fascinating decoration.

The Aragonese, the dynasty that alternated with the Angevin around the middle of the 15th century, tackled the problem of town planning according to a specific programme that reflected the spirit and culture of the Renaissance. The city was enlarged towards the east with the construction of new city walls, most of which are still standing. At the end of the century the kingdom was conquered by Charles VIII of France and, in a brief war between France and Spain, the latter emerged victor for the possession of southern Italy. This is how the long period of Spanish domination began in Naples (1503-1734), bringing with it considerable demographic and housing problems due to the sudden massive influx of noble families of the kingdom, and public officials and soldiers from Spain. The Viceroy, Pedro of Toledo, handled these problems by enlarging the city beyond the Aragonese walls in the west, opening a long boulevard that was named after him, Via Toledo (now Via Roma). Between this road and the hill of Sant'Elmo a dense road network, lined with buildings of the *quarters*, was planned. Despite the decree of 1566 forbidding the construction of new houses outside the city walls, vast new suburbs rose outside the walls.

Triumphal Arch (detail).

Maschio Angioino.

Capri

Its beautiful scenery, the splendour of its panoramic views, its crystal-clear skies and exceptionally mild climate make Capri the most enchanting island in the Neapolitan archipelago. Indeed, it has been called "the island of mermaids" and "pearl of the Bay of Naples": In both winter and spring, it is the most frequently visited island in the Mediterranean, by Italians and foreigners alike, and it is a first-rate tourist centre.

Capri. Panoramic view with the Faraglioni

Piazza del Plebiscito

With the entry of Charles of Bourbon in to Naples in 1734, after a few decades of Austrian domination that had followed Spanish rule, the previous autonomous kingdom was restored, ushering in a period of prosperity with a promising future: the city was a capital once again. Ferdinand IV, who succeeded him in 1759 when Charles became King of Spain, continued his father's policies and was aided by the wise Tanucci, the minister of King Charles. The events of the French Revolution had repercussions on Naples in well, in the brief period of the Parthenopaean Republic from 1798-99. But in 1805, after Napoleon's victory over Austria, a historical period known as the "French decade" began, with the departure of the Bourbons and the installation of Joseph Bonaparte on the throne of the Two Sicilies, followed by Joachim Murat. In 1860, Garibaldi found that in Naples, the way had already been paved for him to conclude his expedition with the annexation to Italy of the Kingdom of the Two Sicilies.

Spaccanapoli Quarter.

SANTA CHIARA

The church of Saint Clare was built at the far end of the gardens of Naples, where Porta Puteolana stood in Greco-Roman times. Commissioned by King Robert of Anjou and his wife Sancha of Majorca to receive the mortal remains of the ruling dynasty, it was built between 1310-1330 by Gagliardo Primario, who alternated soaring Gothic lines with the traditional forms of Latin architecture. In addition to Tino di Camaino, Giovanni and Pacio Bertini da Firenze, Giotto also worked on it, but unfortunately his frescoes have been lost. The plain façade in brown trachyte tuff is preceded by an elegant pronaos covered with a flat roof, with five steep arches; the fourteenth-century marble portal is in the centre under the larger middle one. On the left, the bell tower, built during two periods (1328-43 and 1595), reveals its composite structure. The interior with its single nave ends with the rectangular chancel. Ten chapels with cross vaults illuminated by large Gothic windows, protrude along both sides. The women's galleries are above and double lancet windows rise from the galleries to exalt the soaring vertical lines. The chancel contains the most sumptuous fourteenth-century Italian mausoleum, the tomb of Robert I of Anjou (1343), executed by Giovanni and Pacio Bertini (1433-45).

Church of Santa Chiara. Interior.

Church of Santa Chiara with the sepulchre of Robert I of Anjou, known as "Robert the Wise".

Cloisters of the Poor Clares.

Strozzi Panel.

NATIONAL MUSEUM OF CAPODIMONTE

This museum, along with the archaeological museum and the national library, had its origins in the first group of rich art collections that Charles III of Bourbon inherited from his mother Elisabetta Farnese, the last descendent of the noble family and ambitious consort of the inept Philip V of Spain. The opulent artistic heritage accumulated by Paolo III Farnese and by his descendents arrived in Naples in 1737-38. Initially deposited in the royal palace, the artwork was later moved to several rooms in the hunting lodge that was built by the architects Medrano and Canevari on the orders of Charles III.

Ferdinand IV, his successor, hastened the work, entrusting the building to Fuga and the park and English garden to Sanfelice. The collection subsequently grew with other paintings recovered from the Napoleonic spoils, adding many seventeenth- and eighteenth-century paintings taken from churches and monasteries. The museum includes the Gallery of Eighteenth-century Painting and, on the second floor, the National Gallery.

The following are valuable artistic works: Simone Martini, *Coronation of Robert of Anjou*; Masaccio, *Crucifixion*; Sandro Botticelli, *Madonna and Child with angels*; Correggio, *Zingarella*; Caravaggio, *Flagellation*; Colantonio, *Saint Francis gives the Rule to the Poor Clares* and *Saint Jerome and the Lion*; Sebastiano del Piombo, *Clement VII*; Titian, *Paul III with his nephews Ottavio and Alessandro Farnese*; Pieter Brueghel, *The Misanthrope* and *The Parable of the Blind*.

View of Capodimonte.

NATIONAL ARCHAEOLOGICAL MUSEUM

The building, located in the square of the same name, was built in 1585 as cavalry barracks for the Viceroy, the Duke of Ossuna, who left construction unfinished. Domenico Fontana resumed work in 1616, commissioned by the Viceroy, the Count of Lemnos, who reorganised the statute of the University and established a proper seat for "General Studies". From then until 1777, various courses of higher education were held at this new university site and Giambattista Vico also taught there. Charles III of Bourbon moved the painting and sculpture collection inherited from his mother Elisabetta here, as well as other material of artistic and historical interest from the excavations at Cumae and from other sites in Campania and Apulia. The Picture Gallery has been recently transferred to the Capodimonte Museum. Among the works worth seeing is the group of the *Tyrant-Slayers* in the room of the same name and the *Farnese Athena*; the *Aphrodite "dei Giardini"*; *Orpheus and Eurydice* caught in the pathetic moment of their definitive separation. Room III, the *Doryphorus*, a copy of Polycletus; the *Diomedes* from Cuma; the *Nike* from Naples; the *Farnese Bull*; the *Kallypigos Venus*; the *Aphrodite of Sinuessa*; the *Torso of Venus*. And also, the Herculaneum Gallery, Emperors' Gallery, and the Greek Portrait Gallery. Mosaics Room: the *marine fauna, cockfight, roving musicians and visit to a magician* are remarkable. The mosaic of the *Battle of Issus*, based on an Alexandrian original from the late 4th century B.C. adorned the floor of the tablinum of the House of the Faun at Pompeii. The scene takes place in a restricted space, enlarged through illusion so as to spread out the figures on various planes, with the two leaders emerging from the melee: Alexander, the merciless victor, advances on the left, and with Darius is in the centre where he appears to be preparing to retreat.

National Archaeological Museum.
Aphrodite.

National Archaeological Museum.
Group of the Farnese Bull.

National Archaeological Museum.
Orestes and Electra.

National Archaeological Museum.
Battle of Alexander against Darius.

Pompeii

Pompeii, a town of Oscan origin founded in the 8th century B.C., first entered into the political orbit of Cumae (6th century B.C.), then of the Etruscans, Greeks (474-425) and finally of Rome. During the Social War (91 B.C.) it became a Roman colony. In the city's final days, from 24 to 27 August 79 A.D., the eruption of Vesuvius buried the town under a thick layer (6-7 metres) of molten lava and cinders. Pliny the

Pompeii. Quadrivium of Orpheus

Younger left written description of the eruption and a visit to the excavation site provides further testimony that is no less dramatic. A visit to the ruins of Pompeii gives the impression of an ancient town whose silent life seems to come to life before our very eyes, in the streets, in the shade of the shops, in the homes and in the public buildings. The town, built according to a rational plan within boundary walls, which had 12 towers and 8 gates, is divided by the main E-W roads (decumani) (Via dell'Abbondanza and Via di Nola), by a main N-S road (cardo maximus) (Via Stabiana) and by minor crossroads (cardines) that form 19 regions, each made up of a variable number of blocks of houses (insulae). The following are some particularly important buildings. Antiquarium. The casts of those buried by the eruption are striking. Forum (38 x 142 metres) the centre of activity in the town with the Temple of Jupiter (2nd century B.C.). The covered market or Macellum, the Temple of Vespasian, the Building of Eumachia, the Comitium where elections for public office took place, the Basilica. The Baths of the Forum, The House of the Tragic Poet with the famous mosaic of the dog and the inscription "cave canem". The Via Consolare, the House of Sallust, dating from the Samnite period, the Porta Ercolano gate at the end of Via dei Sepolcri. The Arch of Caligula, with the re-mains of the Temple of Fortuna Augusta built in 3 B.C. in honour of Octavian. The House of the Faun with two atria and two peristyles. From the Arch of Caligula. Via del Mercurio leads to a tower with the same name and is flanked by the Houses of the Great Fountain and the Little Fountain, so named because of the luxurious nymphaeums covered with polychrome mosaics, the House of the Anchor and a tavern (caupona) with interesting paintings in the back-shop. The House of Adonis with the painting that portrays Venus with Adonis wounded and the House of Apollo with paintings. The House of Meleager, a dwelling of the Samnite period, the House of Castor and Pollux, the House of the

Artisan Cherubs.
Pompeii, map.

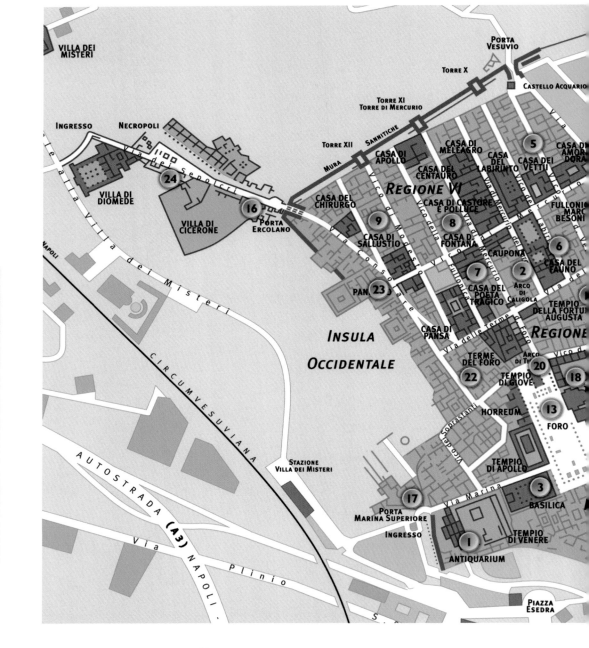

Labyrinth, the House of the Vettii. The house is famous for the splendid paintings in the Fourth Pompeian style. The vestibule leads into the atrium, with an open ceiling (compluvium), an impluvium to collect rainwater, and two strongboxes (arche). On the left is the room with the painting of Ariadne abandoned by Hero and Leander, while Cyparissus, Pan and Cupid, Jupiter, Leda and Danae are portrayed in the next room. In the dining room (triclinium) with the frescoed walls, on a red background divided by pillars are the adventures of Neptune and Amymone, Apollo and Daphne, Bacchus and Ariadne; a series of cupids is portrayed on the cornice of the base. The House of the Gold-

en Cupids for the decoration of the bedroom (cubiculum) with small vitreous discs with cupids carved in gold leaf. All around are finely decorated rooms. Located on Via del Vesuvio are the houses of Orpheus and of the Banker Caecilius Iucundus and the Centenary House. The Central Baths are on Via Stabiana, the vertical axis. Further ahead at n. 5, is the small elegant residence of the priest of the cult of Mars, Marcus Lucretius Fronto, rich with landscape paintings and with a raised

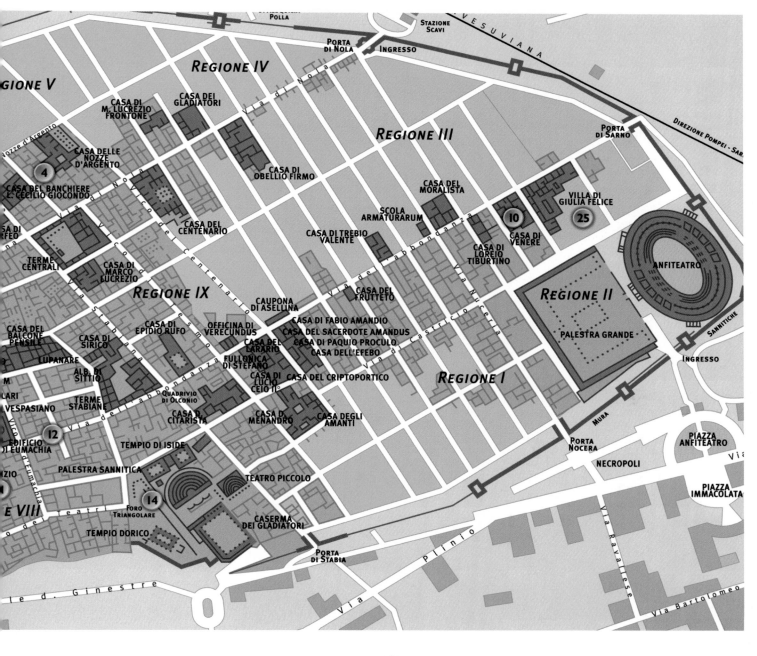

Villa of the Mysteries

VILLA OF THE MYSTERIES

The **Villa of the Mysteries**, built in the 2ⁿᵈ century B.C. and later enlarged, is famous for its splendid frescoes "ad encausto" -encaustic- that adorn the room of the great paintings. The decorations in the Second Pompeian style represent an initiation rite to the mysteries of the cult of Dionysus, against a dark red background on which the figures stand out.

The rite takes place around the central group of Dionysus and Ariadne, from the reading of the ritual to the toilette of the initiate. The warm tones of the colours create a harmonious and rhythmic ensemble. Among the most fascinating details are the figures of the bride and of the priestess, whose dancing is airily emphasised by the cape falling from her shoulders.

Pompeii. Great Theatre.

garden adorned with statues and then the House of Siricus (n. 23). Opposite the Olconio crossroads (quadrivium), a right turn onto Via dell'Abbondanza (a decumanus) leads to the grand Stabian Baths. In the vast palaestra surrounded on three sides by an arcade, various rooms are divided, as was the custom, into male and female sections. Vaults and walls are decorated with beautiful coloured stuccowork from the Flavian period. The Triangular Forum, around which are grouped public and religious buildings of the Hellenistic period. The Great Theatre is next to it. The Gladiators' Barracks. In Via Stabiana is the small temple of Jupiter Meilichios. At the Quadrivium of Holconius, the House of the Lararium. The House of Loreius Tiburtinus, the House of Venus, and lastly the residence of Julia Felix.

Pompeii. Building of Eumachia.

RIACE BRONZES

The artist who moulded these two statues, whose names remain unknown, seems to have lived around the 5th century B.C. These bronzes are about 2 metres high and are in the National Museum of Reggio Calabria. The works, of great artistic value, were discovered in 1972 at the bottom of the sea in front of Riace, recovered and shipped to Florence to be cleaned of the encrustations and restored in the Workshop of Semiprecious stones. Based on a study of the position of the heads and arms, these works can probably be dated to around the mid-5th century B.C.

National Museum
of Reggio Calabria. Riace Bronzes.

Sicily

Starting in the 9th century B.C. various peoples emigrated to the island of Sicily from the cities of Greece, and from the islands and coasts of the Mediterranean. In the search for new sites near their places of origin, the navigators chose accessible ports and natural bays. The Phoenicians occupied the western coastline, the Greeks the eastern one, and the cities of Palermo, Agrigento, Gela and Syracuse were founded. The struggle between the Carthaginians and the Greeks lasted for several centuries, until the Tyrant Dionysius asserted the supremacy

Taormina with the Greek theatre and view of Etna.

of Syracuse over Sicily, along the coast to the Gulf of Naples where Cumae was founded. Caere was conquered along the coasts of the Etruscans and its temple plundered of its rich votive works, while the Dalmatian and Italian coasts were also conquered and Adria was built. The court of Dionysius was a renowned centre of culture that was also visited by Plato, where the philosopher ran the risk of being sold as a slave, and by other poets such as Pindar, Aeschylus, Simonides and Bacchylides. However, the rule of the tyrants was not destined to last. With the Roman conquest, cities underwent transformations and only small parts remained intact. Roman rule was followed by Byzantine, Arab, Norman, and Swabian domination. From the Swabian period it is worth remembering the fortresses of Frederick II, with a polygonal shape and a metaphysical aura, such as the one of Andria built in Apulia, the most famous and frequently visited. Under this great emperor, the arts and sciences flourished. The Spanish occupation and unification with Italy followed.

PALERMO

Palermo is a city with a very ancient tradition, as demonstrated by its monuments and findings. The Phoenicians gave it the name of "all port" and named it "Ziz", flower. The Carthaginians fortified it between the 8th-7th century B.C. and in 254 B.C. it was conquered by Rome. With their occupation in 827, the Arabs transformed it into a cultural, economic and political capital. In 1072, it was seized by the Normans and later by the Swabians, under which it reached the height of its splendour with Frederick II. From 1415 to 1713, Sicily was a part of the Spanish kingdom. The figure of Garibaldi and the Unification of Italy stand out in the successive events involving the island.

A tour of Palermo offers a view of several interesting buildings. The Palace of the Normans, or Royal Palace that Roger II enlarged and embellished. The King's Room with its cross vault covered with mosaics depicting hunting scenes,

Palermo. San Giovanni degli Eremiti.

Palermo. La Martorana Church.

and the Palatine Chapel (1130) with its fine mosaic decoration are renowned. The tombs of Roger II, Frederick II, Constance of Altavilla and Constance of Aragona are preserved in the Cathedral.

San Giovanni degli Eremiti, the complex with church and monastery, built between 1142 and 1148. The Palazzo della "Zisa" (from aziz, or splendid) built under William I and William II. The Church of San Cataldo (mid-12th century), with small raised domes in the typical Norman style. The Church of the Martorana, which is recommended for its mosaic decorations.

Via Maqueda is the main street, which is crossed by Corso Vittorio Emanuele to form - with Piazza Vigliena - the Four Corners of the city. The four marble statues represent the seasons, while the others portray the Spanish kings and patron saints. Piazza Pretoria is surrounded by Palazzo delle Aquile (1463-1478), seat of the Commune of Palermo, the entrance to San Giuseppe dei Teatini and Piazza dei Quattro Canti. The fountain was made in Florence by Francesco Camilliani and Michelangelo Naccherino. The Regional Archaeological Museum is recommended for the metopes from temples at Selinus. Palazzo Abatellis or Patella, which houses the Sicilian Regional Gallery, was built between 1490 and 1495 on a plan by Matteo Carnelivari. The pilgrimage to Mount Pellegrino to the Sanctuary of St. Rosalie, the beautiful niece of the Norman King Roger of Altavilla should not be missed.

Monreale. Aerial view.

Monreale. Cathedral.

MONREALE

William II - William the Good - had the cathedral, convent and royal palace built. The church, dedicated to Our Lady of the Assumption, is Romanesque, Byzantine and Islamic. The Cathedral is crowned with two dissimilar towers and in the centre of the façade there are three arches with Doric columns. The façade of the apse is covered with interlaced arches, small columns with capitals and tiles of lava and limestone that form geometrical motifs of Islamic inspiration.

The doorway of the main entrance (1186) is the work of Bonanno Pisano: it has intaglios and strips of mosaic, marble sculptures and bronze doors, which have 42 panels with episodes taken from the Old Testament sculpted in relief. The left portal, by Barisano da Trani, dated from 1179, shows figures of saints in the 28 panels. The portal is protected by the portico of Giovanni and Fazo Gagini (16th century).

The interior of the square cathedral is in a Latin cross, with naves marked by columns and pointed arches, typical of Arab architecture. The double-sloped roof of the nave has exposed painted beams and the ceiling of the chancel reflects Muslim influence. The floor is in white Taormina marble, porphyry and granite. The walls above and the ceiling are decorated with 6,400 sq. m. of mosaics. The 130 paintings were executed between the second half of the 12th century and the first half of the 13th with episodes taken from the Old and New Testaments. The cloister, preserved intact, is embellished with 228 twin columns, each in a different material with gold inlay, precious stones, lava and mosaics. Each capital shows biblical scenes, pagan myths, animals and natural motifs. The most valued is the small cloister with the fountain in the shape of a stylised palm tree.

Taormina. Isola Bella.

TAORMINA

The city rises on a wonderful site. It was founded by a group of Greek refugees in the 4th century B.C. The Romans left their mark on the town plan, and with the Byzantines it became the capital of eastern Sicily. During the 10th-11th century it was destroyed by the Arabs. The Greek theatre is the symbol of the town. Built in the 3rd century B.C., it is dug entirely out of rock; it is 50 metres wide, 120 long and 20 high (only the one in Syracuse is larger). The Roman Theatre, the Odeon, is smaller than the Greek one. The Cathedral (13th century) dedicated to St. Nicholas is the most important church in the town. The interior in the shape of a Latin cross has a nave and two aisles divided by two rows of three columns each, in pink Taormina marble, with leaf-decorated capitals. In the nave the ceiling has exposed beams supported by corbels carved with arabesque motifs. The polyptych by Antonello de Saliba (16th century) is interesting. Palazzo Corvaia was built and enlarged in later periods: the cubic tower and the central part go back to the Arabs, the left side wing to the 13th century, and the remainder was built in the 15th century. The façade is impressive, and inside there are wonderful relief panels with episodes from the Book of Genesis.

"I don't believe in Hell very much but I do believe in Paradise because I've seen it, and this is it".

Edmondo De Amicis

CATANIA

The Romans conquered Catania in 263 B.C. and built the Roman Theatre on the south slope of the hill. The lower part of the structure is now flooded with water from the Amenano River. The Odeon is an edifice built in brick, marble and lava stone; the hemicycle is composed of 18 walls that form 17 rooms covered with vaults.

The Cathedral is divided into a nave and two aisles and the sixteenth-century wooden choir can still be seen in the central apse. The tomb of the patron saint of the city, St. Agatha, is in the chapel named after her. The chapels of the towers contain the remains of Constance of Aragona and other Aragonese sovereigns. The tomb of Vincenzo Bellini is set against the second column. Catania was destroyed by an earthquake and rebuilt in 1693.

Empedocles *(492-430 B.C.)*

He was a famous scientist and is recognised as the founder of the Italian School of Medicine. Fire, air, water, and earth are the elements that make up the base of his theory of physics. Love and Strife contribute by nearing and moving away from the creation of life. Knowledge is feeling.

Rome. Raphael Rooms, Signatura Room, The School of Athens.
Portrait of Empedocles

Temple of Concord.

AGRIGENTO
VALLEY OF TEMPLES

It was one of the last Greek colonies to be founded in 580 B.C., in the inspiring Valley of Temples. Conquered by the Arabs in 827, it was adorned with mosques and under their rule trade flourished in the city, called Kerkent. The Normans took control of it two centuries later. The philosopher Empedocles was one of the leading figures born in this city.

Temple of Heracles.

The buildings in the Valley of Temples are in the Doric style, with the exception of the Temple of Heracles, in the Doric-Archaic style. The temples have six columns along the short side, and a single row around the cella where the statue of the deity was set opposite the main entrance, facing east so it would be illuminated by the rays of the rising sun, the symbol of life.

The San Nicola Archaeological Museum is one of the most interesting for its rare collection of terracottas, which were votive offerings hung on the walls of the temple, and for the rare finds recovered in the vicinity, such as the Ephebus and the Telamon.

The **Temple of Concord** was built in 430 B.C. and it is virtually intact. The 34 impressive tapered columns set around its perimeter are seven metres high. The frieze is decorated with triglyphs and metopes. The **Temple of Zeus** was one of the most popular places of worship in the ancient world: 113 metres long and 56 metres wide, it had columns that soared to a height of 20 metres, alternated with giant Telamons or Atlases. It was built to celebrate the victory over Carthage in 480 B.C. The **Temple of Castor and Pollux** was built in the mid-5th century B.C. in honour of the twins born from Zeus and Leda, Queen of Sparta.

The **Temple of Heracles,** built in the 6th century B.C., is believed to be the oldest.

Archimedes *(287-212 B.C.)*

Mathematician and researcher, he was killed by a Roman soldier. A stone with a sphere inscribed in a cylinder to remember the studies that he carried out on this figure was placed on his tomb. He is attributed with the invention of a burning mirror with which he is said to have set Roman ships on fire.

Rome. Raphael Rooms, Signatura Room, The School of Athens.
Portrait of Archimedes

SYRACUSE

Castle of Euryelus.

The city of Syracuse was founded on the small island of Ortygia in 734 B.C. It developed over the years and became progressively more powerful, ultimately fighting and defeating Carthage and Athens. The conquest of the city came when Dionysius the Elder ushered in a fortunate period. At the time Syracuse was surrounded with enormous walls, had a population greater than that of Athens, was defended by an army made up of soldiers of fortune - Etruscans and Lombards - and was respected and feared by the peoples of other cities. Its illustrious figures include Archimedes (287-212), Sophron, Epicharmus, and Theocritus. Conquered by the Romans in 212, and then sacked by the Franks and Goths, it subsequently fell under Arab and then Byzantine rule, and in 1086 it was conquered by the Normans and Swabians. They were followed by the Angevin, Aragonese, Castilian and Hapsburg royal families. The Bourbons, Savoy and Austrians also ruled there.

The Cathedral of Syracuse originated from the transformation in Byzantine times of the Temple of Athena (5th century B.C.) or Athenaion. It had six columns on the shorter end and fourteen on its sides, and the columns were over eight metres high. The interior of the cathedral has a nave and two side aisles with numerous chapels on the side of the right aisle. Opposite the church is the Senate Building, built in 1629 based on plans by Giovanni Vermexio. The Fountain of Arethusa has been the symbol of Syracuse since ancient times: it is an extraordinary spring of fresh water that flows directly into the sea.

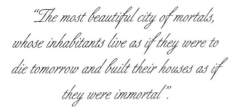

"The most beautiful city of mortals, whose inhabitants live as if they were to die tomorrow and built their houses as if they were immortal".

Pindar, 5ᵗʰ century B.C.

At the entry to the island of Ortygia rises the Temple of Apollo, built in the first half of the 6th century B.C. The Greek theatre of Syracuse, dating from the 5ᵗʰ century B.C., is the largest monolithic theatre, as it is entirely hewn in solid rock. The Altar of Hieron II is the largest sacrificial altar in Greek history, and it was commissioned by the Tyrant Hieron II in the 3ʳᵈ century B.C. It is almost 200 metres long and 23 wide. The Ear of Dionysius is an artificial grotto that is 65 metres long and 23 high, and it was used by Dionysius to incarcerate political prisoners. The Castle of Euryelus is all that remains of the massive fortifications commissioned by Dionysius the Elder in 402 B.C.

They included 27 kilometres of walls and an impressive fortress with galleries, drawbridge, traps and moats. The Roman amphitheatre was built between the 4ᵗʰ and 2ⁿᵈ century B.C. Gladiators fights with wild beasts and naval battles were organised there.

The Roman sarcophagus of Adelphia, carved in bas-relief with 62 figures drawn from the Old and New Testament, was found in the Catacombs of St. John of the 4ᵗʰ and 5ᵗʰ century. The Castle of Maniace was commissioned in 1235 by Frederick II of Swabia. The Paolo Orsi Regional Archaeological Museum is interesting for the section dedicated to Greek Syracuse and its colonies, and the most important pieces include the Anadiomene Venus and the sarcophagus of Adelphia. The Giudecca was the area of the island of Ortygia inhabited by Jews.

Fountain of Arethusa.

Greek Theatre.

Piazza Armerina. Villa del Casale.
Villa del Casale. Mosaic

PIAZZA ARMERINA
VILLA DEL CASALE

Built between the 3rd and 4th century A.D. it was probably the residence of a tetrarch or the summer villa of an emperor. The plan of the building is organised on various levels according to the characteristics of terrace constructions. Its rooms can be grouped into four areas: entry and thermal water rooms, the peristyle that also included the main room and rooms for guests, private quarters and basilica, and finally the triclinium and the elliptical court.

Splendid mosaics cover the flooring of the villa for a total area of over 3,500 sq.m. Their execution can be attributed to African masters, who used a style marked by profound realism to depict the daily life of ancient Rome, scenes from the works of Homer, and mythological episodes. In the vestibule, the subject of the mosaic portrays several servants welcoming guests. Medallions with animal heads are displayed in the large rectangular peristyle.

The hunting motif is present in many other rooms: the Room of the Little Hunt shows hunters, followed by dogs and servants, who are offering sacrifices to Diana. In the Hall of the Great Hunt, the mosaic covers an area of 350 sq. m. This area is followed by the palaestra, the dancing room with dancers; the dining room decorated with a series of scenes of the cycle of Hercules and lastly the baths.

Selinus. Temple E.

Noto. Natural Oasis

SELINUS

Founded in 651-650 B.C. or in 627 B.C., Selinus rose on a promontory, at the mouth of the navigable rivers, Selinos and Cottone. where two ports were built. During the wars, Selinus followed a pro-Phoenician and pro-Punic policy: in 480 B.C. it allied with Carthage against the Greeks in the Battle of Himera. In 409 B.C., however, it was taken by storm and destroyed by the Carthaginian army. The same Carthaginians sought to destroy it during the First Punic War, so it would not fall into the hands of the Romans.

The following temples are named with letters of the alphabet to distinguish them. Temple G, dedicated to Zeus (530-409 B. C.) was one of the largest temples of ancient times. Temple F was dedicated to Athena. Temple E was dedicated to Hera (5th century B.C.).

The Sanctuary of Malophoros was part of a group of temples and is formed by two sacred areas. In all likelihood this temple was dedicated to Demeter,

Temple C was built towards the mid-6th century B.C. Temple D stands north of Temple C; it was 56 metres long and the 78 columns, which formed the perimeter were 7.5 metres high. Temple Y or the Temple of the Small Metopes is interesting for the six metopes that portray the "*Rape of Europa*", the "*Winged Sphinx'*", "*Hercules fighting the bull*", "*Demeter, Kore and Hecate*", a biga and the "*Triad of Athens*", or Apollo, Artemis and Latona. Temple A and Temple O also stand on the acropolis.

Noto

Ancient Noto, or Neai, was founded by the Siculi and was conquered by the Greeks and Romans. It was razed to the ground on 11 January 1693 and reconstructed by the Duke of Camastra on a plan by several Sicilian architects. The present-day appearance of Noto is characterised by the Baroque style, like the façade of the Cathedral of St. Nicholas. Other buildings are the Monastery; the Basilica and the Seminary of the Holy Saviour, Palazzo Landolina and Palazzo Ducezio. Visitors should be sure to see the springtime "Infiorata" - decorations made with petals - on Via Nicolaci. Palazzo Nicolaci is famous for the variety of its balconies.

JEWS AND SYNAGOGUES

The first ghetto in Italy was founded in Venice in 1516. Various "scole" - or synagogues - were built subsequently: the Grande Scola Tedesca, the Scola Levantina in 1538 and several others. The ghetto was named after the furnaces where metal was melted down to make weapons, and it became the area where the Jews were forced to live. Entry and exit from the ghetto was established by the ringing of a bell. However, the Jews were authorised to exercise various professions, working as street vendors or moneylenders. Over the centuries the Jews became a large and active community, as literary works such as "The Merchant of Venice" by Shakespeare testify. In 1800, the Jews obtained their freedom and mixed with the population living in various parts of the city.

In Florence the area inhabited by the Jews was the area of the present-day Piazza della Repubblica. They were supported by the Medici family, who recognised their commercial importance. The ancient synagogues of Florence no longer exist. The Jewish Centre is now located at Via Farini, 4.

The Jewish community of Rome is the oldest in Italy and the Jews were continuously subjected to the will of whoever held power. In the 13th century the Jews had to wear a small yellow circle as a badge and they had to pay a tax to organise certain celebrations. With the Counter-Reformation, the position of the Jews in the city became more restrictive due to the rigid and intransigent attitude of the popes. Several "scole" were located in the ghetto including three Italian, one Catalan and one Castilian. Rome now has a permanent exhibition of the Jewish community.

Syracuse. The Giudecca was the area of the island of Ortygia inhabited by Jews. The most important community of the Jewish faith goes back to the second half of the 14th century and for all of the following century, until in 1492 Ferdinand II of Spain decided to expel them from the kingdom. The oldest miqwé in the western Mediterranean was recently discovered in Casa Bianca. It was a bath of purification that women were subjected to in order to free themselves from impurities.

Venice. Old Ghetto. Synagogue.

Rome. Lungotevere Cenci.

Florence. Synagogue.